The Giving Gift

Filiae, Filioque

For Mary and David

The Giving Gift

The Holy Spirit in Person

TOM SMAIL

Wipf & Stock
PUBLISHERS
Eugene, Oregon

Wipf and Stock Publishers
199 W 8th Ave, Suite 3
Eugene, OR 97401

The Giving Gift
The Holy Spirit in Person
By Smail, Thomas A.
Copyright©1994 by Smail, Thomas A.
ISBN: 1-59244-987-5
Publication date 11/2/2004
Previously published by Darton, Longman, and Todd, 1994

Contents

A Hymn for the Baptism of Jesus

Father, behold your Son made man
  To baptism comes in Jordan's stream,
And thus fulfils your ancient plan
  All Adam's children to redeem.
    Your voice from heaven your will attests,
    "My Son, on whom my favour rests."

Blest Spirit, who in Mary's womb
  The new humanity began,
Who soon from Joseph's darkened tomb
  Will bring to life the Son of Man,
    The baptised Christ with gifts endow,
    Anoint the new Messiah now.

Lord Jesus Christ, now Son proclaimed,
  Baptised with Holy Spirit's powers,
Unsullied Lamb of God now named,
  The sins you bear, not yours but ours,
    Go forth the Devil's wrath to face
    Live, die and rise to save our race.

O Triune God, your people claim,
  The Father's children by his grace,
Those who confess the Son's great name,
  The Holy Spirit's dwelling place,
    Your baptised Church in faith will pray,
    Your threefold glory now display!

This hymn may be sung to the tune *Surrey* which is in most of the standard books. General permission for its use in worship is hereby granted provided that the words are unchanged and that no commercial use is made of them.

Preface to the Second Edition

The purpose of this book is to explore in a reasonably accessible way the interface between the renewing work of the Holy Spirit, which many in our own day have been experiencing in new ways, and the classical trinitarian tradition of the Church and its theology, in the conviction that each has much to gain by attending to and learning from the other.

In isolation from an experienced relationship to Father, Son and Holy Spirit, trinitarian theology can easily get lost in its own complicated abstractions that have little obvious relevance to or connection with the ongoing life of most Christian communities, but, on the other hand, a one-sided absorption in dramatic spiritual experiences can easily obscure the fact that the purpose of the Spirit's coming is to relate us to the Father and the Son. Against that danger a good trinitarian theology can act as a necessary and valuable corrective.

Those involved in spiritual renewal have in recent years been becoming increasingly aware that trinitarian theology is not an optional extra for those with intellectual pretensions, but an important tool by which we can measure and adjust contemporary experience to make sure that the thrust and balance of the given biblical gospel is being maintained.

Alongside this, mainstream theology has in recent decades been showing a new and very fruitful awareness of the centrality of the doctrine of the Trinity as the distinctive Christian statement about God as he has revealed himself in Christ, and in particular there has been a fresh and creative encounter between the understanding of that doctrine in the

Western and Eastern Churches, from which I have learnt much. The title itself gives ample evidence of my continued indebtedness to the tradition of Augustine but the book itself makes clear that we in the Christian West have a very great deal to learn from the Cappadocian fathers of the Eastern Church and their modern Orthodox successors.

I believe that it will be much to the health of those involved in the renewal movements of our day to anchor themselves afresh in trinitarian theology, and equally to the good of the theologians to realise that God the Holy Trinity is to be encountered and worshipped before he can be rightly thought about. This book is intended as a very modest contribution to that process of cross fertilisation.

The book was conceived when I was teaching doctrine in St John's College Nottingham, developed during a memorable month at St Paul's College, Grahamstown, South Africa, and given final form while I was a parish priest in Sanderstead, South Croydon and it owes much to all three.

The central subject of the book is the distinct personhood of the Holy Spirit and, in an area where one cannot but be aware of vast horizons and unfathomed depths, I have had to restrict myself to what was directly relevant to that central concern.

As I have read and thought around the subject I have become more and more convinced, certainly of the incompleteness but even more of the basic correctness of the central core of classical Christian teaching about the Trinity and the Spirit. If in our days we are to do something about the incompleteness it will be by going on from what we have inherited from our fathers and not by going back on it. The intention of this work is to join with the Church catholic, orthodox, reformed and charismatic in its praise and proclamation of the triune name of the God who is Father, Son and Holy Spirit, to whom be glory for ever.

Special thanks are due to Mary Duncan who corrected the proofs, to Alan Royou who drew the diagrams and to my wife and family who allowed me room to write.

London, Trinity 1994

Chapter One

Beginning with Mary

I nearly called this book, 'What the charismatic renewal did not say about the Holy Spirit.' That at any rate would have had the merit of making it clear right from the start that it is not a book about the central charismatic concerns and not much will be found in it about baptism in the Spirit or spiritual gifts such as tongues, prophecy and healing. I have often had my say on such matters and have little more to add. Such a title, however, would have failed to indicate that it is only because of the charismatic renewal that I am writing about the Holy Spirit at all. I believe firmly that he has been at work in my life since my baptism as an infant right at its beginning, but I also know that I became aware of him in a new way in the renewal of my life and ministry that resulted from my contact with the early charismatic renewal in November 1965, and that my taking him seriously both in my thinking and living began at that point.

So, as a confessed and continuing debtor to the renewal movement, I want nevertheless to press on beyond it. My attitude to it nowadays is very much like that of the writer to the Hebrews when he wrote, 'Let us leave the elementary teachings... and go on to maturity, not laying again the foundation of repentance from acts that lead to death, and of faith in God, instructions about baptisms, the laying on of hands, the resurrection of the dead and eternal judgment' (Hebrews 6:1-2).

To which it might justly have been retorted that there are many who lack just that foundation and cannot build anything until it has been securely laid. In the same way contemporary charismatics might rightly argue that people cannot become mature in the Spirit until they have begun in the Spirit, and to lead them to such a beginning is a highly relevant and indeed urgently necessary ministry today.

My own questionings about the renewal movement do not concern its ability under God to rejuvenate churches and Christians but rather its ability to mature what it has rejuvenated. However that may be, there is an abundance of literature about being renewed in the Spirit, but not so much about being matured in the Spirit, and because the latter is my own present need and concern, it is also the subject of this book. If it is undoubtedly true that it was through 'baptisms and the laying on of hands' that we were first touched by the Spirit, it is equally true that we must 'go on to maturity' by becoming concerned not just with how and when we were touched but with the one who touched us, with the Holy Spirit himself, not just in the narrow perspective of charismatic gifts but in all dimensions of his activity in the life of God, of the Church and of the world.

What I am searching for in this book is some starting point for a mature understanding of the Holy Spirit that does justice not only to his more dramatic manifestations but to all the work he was sent to do. To find that breadth of understanding we must look primarily to the witness of Scripture and also to the evidence of two thousand years of Christian tradition and of the experience of countless believers. At the same time we need to probe beyond his work to his person. What Jesus did always raised the question as to who Jesus was. In the same way to experience the work of the Spirit leads us to ask whose work it is; openness to and enjoyment of the gifts creates a concern with the giver of these gifts. It is strange that among all the many books that have appeared in the last twenty years about the activity of the Spirit, hardly any so much as glance at the question of his person. Even so theologically aware a writer as Dr James Packer in *Keep in Step with the Spirit*[1] has next to nothing to say about why we need to confess the Spirit as a third divine person along with the Father and the Son. The fact that the subject is elusive and difficult does not mean that it is not very important and we propose to redress the balance by making the person of the Spirit our central theme.

In case anyone should think that all this is a merely academic or purely theoretical exercise, let it be said at once that our aim is pre-eminently practical. The importance of a mature understanding of the Holy Spirit is that it will help to produce a more mature Church. The main reason for a concern with his person is that we should be more open to the whole range of his promises and how they relate to the gospel as a whole, and so more able to pray for his living presence to enable us to grow up into all the riches of Christ that he brings to us.

In recent years I have often found myself saying that the primary work of the Holy Spirit in the New Testament does not have to do with charismatic manifestations but with our initiation into the two central relationships that are summed up in the two confessions, 'Abba, Father' and 'Jesus is Kurios, Lord'. Before the Spirit relates us to one another in love or to the world in missionary outreach, he relates us to God the Father and God the Son in worshipping acknowledgment of who they are for us. Central to Paul's teaching about the Spirit is the statement in I Corinthians 12:3 that 'no one can say "Jesus is Lord," except by the Holy Spirit', and the other statement in Galatians 4:6, 'Because you are sons, God sent the Spirit of his Son into our hearts, the Spirit who calls out "Abba, Father".' To bring us into relationship to the Jesus who is Kurios (Lord) and the God who is Abba (Father) is the primary charismatic work of the Spirit. Without his gracious activity, such relationships and the confession of them would remain impossible to us. It is to those who know and confess Kurios and Abba that the Spirit imparts his gifts and pours out his love. A Christian becomes charismatic – that is, enters the dynamic field of the Spirit's action – not when he speaks in tongues and prophesies but when he confesses Kurios and Abba.

That at once makes clear that the action of the Spirit extends to the whole God-man, Christ-Christian relationships and not just one part of them and it raises the question of what precisely the role of the Spirit is in creating and maintaining these relationships. It suggests further that the Holy Spirit operates in a trinitarian context: his work is to relate us to the Father and the Son, because the Spirit himself in his own being is intimately related to both the Father and the Son. We must ask how, as the third trinitarian person who relates us to the other two, he is himself related to the Father and the Son. Questions like this lie before us, but we can see from the outset clear indications that the work and person of the Spirit can be explicated only in the context of a trinitarian doctrine of God. The texts we have just quoted, and especially Galatians 4:6 (cf II Corinthians 13:14) strongly suggest that it was in an implicitly trinitarian context that the Holy Spirit was originally received, so that it will be only in the same context that all that he does and is can be rightly understood.

We shall therefore be asking how the distinctive work of the Spirit in salvation and creation is to be understood in its connection with and distinction from the work of the Father and the Son, and how therefore the person of the Spirit is to be understood in its connection with and distinction from the persons of the Father and the Son. Put more simply: How does what he does relate to what they do, and how does who he is relate to who they are?

The Spirit as Giving Gift

We may give a preliminary answer to both these questions in terms of our title by saying that the Holy Spirit is the Giving Gift. First question: What does the Holy Spirit do within the God-man relationship? Answer: He gives the things of God and the things of Christ to us. Second question: Who is the Holy Spirit? Answer: Within the God-man relationship he is the one who is given to us primarily by the Father and secondarily by the Son (both adverbs needing explanation), and, within the life of God himself, he is primarily the Gift of the Father to the Son and secondarily the responsive Gift of the Son to the Father. The whole of what follows is an explanation of these two questions and answers.

The important thing to notice at this point is that the idea of the Spirit as Giving Gift is central to the whole case we shall be developing. It is a notion that is significant for three different reasons:

1. It shows that we are still in continuity with the basic insights of the charismatic renewal. The Greek word *charisma* means free gift of grace, and the renewal has regularly spoken of the Spirit as the giver of many gifts as well as being himself God's Gift to us. In a more fundamental and extended way, we are saying the same thing still.

2. Even more importantly, in describing the Spirit in this way we are using categories that have for centuries been traditional, especially in the Church of the West. Augustine in the fourth century and Thomas Aquinas in the thirteenth century both note that one of the difficulties we face when we try to speak about the Spirit is that the word Spirit can be used either to speak of the third person of the Trinity or to speak of the whole Godhead. So you can quite well say that the Father and the Son are Spirit or, with John's gospel, that God himself is Spirit (John 4:24). So the term Spirit, as well as being the distinctive name of the third person of the Trinity, can be used as a general term to describe the 'stuff' of which, so to speak, God is made, the dynamic, free, self-giving divine life that belongs equally to all three divine persons.

Therefore, as Augustine and Thomas argued, we need another term to describe what is specific to, and distinctive of, the third person of the Trinity over against the other two. For this purpose they, and the whole western catholic tradition that they shaped, thought of the Spirit as Gift. Father and Son are, each in his own way, the givers, and the Spirit is the Gift that they give. Father and Son are God as giver, the Holy Spirit is God as Gift. In the relationship between God and man, Father and Son stand on one side of the relationship as the givers, and we stand on the other as the beneficiaries of their giving. The gift itself, or rather the Gift himself is the Holy Spirit who originally belongs with the Father and the Son on the divine side of the relationship, but who passes across to our side, just as a gift passes from the donor to the recipient. Thus the Holy Spirit is God as given to us, God who is with us and in us on our side of our relationship with the Father and the Son – he is God as given, God the Gift.

To put the same thing another way, if we analyse the sentence, 'God gives himself to us', the active subject, 'God', refers to the Father and the Son as, each in his own way, a giver of the Spirit, whereas 'himself' refers to the Holy Spirit, who is also God, but God as given to us.

All this will become clearer as we proceed. We shall have more than one serious question to put to the Augustine-Thomas way of thinking about the Spirit, but in understanding him as fundamentally God who is given to us by God the Father through God the Son and who is therefore God as Gift, we shall be affirming the basic approach of that tradition.

3. Most importantly of all, to describe the Holy Spirit as Gift has a firm basis in the New Testament itself. For example, in his Pentecost sermon, Peter tells the people what God is ready to do for those who repent and come to faith in Christ. He promises that along with the forgiveness of their sins they will receive 'the gift of the Holy Spirit' (Acts 2:38). The Spirit himself is the primary gift of God to believers. Before we are given particular gifts of the Spirit, we are given the Spirit himself as the source of all the rest. He is the Gift who gives – the Giving Gift. This is the gift that, when the apostles came to Samaria, Simon the magician tried to buy with money, and Peter had to make it clear that the Spirit is not up for sale to the highest bidder: he is the 'gift of God' (Acts 8:20) who is freely given – in this case through the laying on of the apostles' hands. He comes whenever and to whomsoever God is pleased to give him, and not when all sorts of prior conditions have been fulfilled.

He even comes where the apostles did not expect or even want him to come. For example, he falls on Cornelius and his friends and Peter is amazed and even scandalised to discover that 'the gift of the Holy Spirit had been poured out even on the Gentiles' (Acts 10:45).

This way of thinking about the Spirit is not confined to Luke/Acts. In John's gospel Jesus offers the woman of Samaria 'living water', one of John's favourite ways of speaking about the Spirit (cf John 7:37). Jesus says, 'If you knew the gift of God and who it is that asks you for a drink, you would have asked him and he would have given you living water' (John 4:10). The gift of God is the living water which is the Holy Spirit. In the same way Hebrews 6:4 describes Christians as those 'who have tasted the heavenly gift, who have shared in the Holy Spirit'. It is clear that the second phrase explains the first. To share in the Holy Spirit is to take into yourself the gift of God.

In all these passages the Greek word used for gift is *dórea*, a word that specially emphasises the sheer graciousness of the act of giving. The phrase *dórea tou Theou*, gift of God, complements the phrase, *dórea tou Pneumatos Hagiou*, gift of the Holy Spirit. God is the donor and the Holy Spirit is that which he gives. Many other texts could be quoted in which the Holy Spirit is the object of the verb 'to give' or the verb 'to receive', showing that the basic idea of the Spirit as Gift that is given by God and received by us is a familiar and central one for many of the New Testament writers.

So, to think of the Spirit as Gift has a good foundation in Scripture, in classical catholic tradition and in modern charismatic experience. There is, therefore, good hope that it will provide a fruitful starting point for our own enquiry. Even now, we can set out three affirmations that are closely connected with the idea of the Spirit as Gift and will be with us throughout the book.

Three Basic Affirmations

1. To describe the Holy Spirit as Gift emphasises that we are here in the realm of grace. Free giving is not by any means the only kind of exchange that can take place between two parties. A cheque can pass from me to you as a contracted payment of wages in return for services rendered. It is then not a gift but a payment, a *quid pro quo* in which one party

fulfils agreed conditions and the other party is in duty bound
to pay the agreed reward.

Some Christians have tended to understand God's sending
of the Holy Spirit in this contractual way. God gives the
Spirit when we fulfil the conditions that he has laid down.
This view has both a typically Roman Catholic and a
typically Protestant form.

In much traditional Catholic spirituality the full indwelling of the Holy Spirit is seen as the reward of a long
laborious effort after sanctity, so that the gifts and fruit of the
Spirit are the end product of an extended process of
disciplined prayer, stern self-denial and costly strivings for
holiness, perhaps in a monastic setting. They are thus the
prerogatives of the saints and indeed the signs and proofs of
their sainthood.

The Catholic charismatic renewal has rebelled against that
approach. What was seen as a reward for the few who could
attain to the heights of holiness, is now seen as a gift freely
offered to all who belong to Christ and indeed implicit in
their baptismal initiation into his grace. What was once shut
up in the cloister has been set free in a popular movement.
Once more the Spirit is seen not as a reward for the few but as
a free gift to the many. Far from being a reversal of Catholic
tradition, this is a return to its basic insight that God lavishes
his Spirit and his gifts on his people not in proportion to their
achievements but in the freedom of his mercy and grace.

The Protestant form of the same contractual approach is
deeply entrenched in much denominational pentecostalism
and often shows itself in the mainline charismatic renewal. It
holds that the Spirit and his gifts are given when we have
repented enough, prayed enough, claimed enough, 'tarried'
enough.[2]

Such an approach almost inevitably leads to a pre-
occupation with ourselves and how we can receive the Spirit,
rather than with God and his willingness to give the Spirit. It
can also threaten the very notion that the Spirit is Gift. What
sort of a gift is it that can be bestowed only when required
conditions have been fulfilled? It is a bit like the 'free gifts'
offered by the cornflakes' manufacturers to induce us to buy

their product. It is in fact neither gift nor free, because the value of the gift is included in the cost of the product. That may be good trade but it is bad theology. God does not extract a hidden payment for his gifts. His gifts have life-changing consequences, but no preconditions, except the willingness to receive them. In the New Testament, as we shall see, even that willingness is regarded as itself a gift of God rather than a precondition for receiving a gift.

If that is true of all God's gifts, it is supremely true of his supreme Gift, the Holy Spirit. In his Pentecost sermon Peter offers that Gift to potential converts as part of the beginning of their Christian life (Acts 2:38). The faith and repentance with which the Gift is to be received are not things that his Jewish hearers have to produce out of themselves as their entitlement to the Spirit. Their willingness to turn round to Christ and hold out empty hands for what Peter is promising has been produced in them by the word Peter has preached in the power of the Spirit, by which they 'were cut to the heart' (v 37). So it was the Spirit who made them open to the Spirit: their faith and repentance were themselves his work and gift.

Our sinful hearts are for ever trying to turn the good news of God's grace into a series of daunting demands for us to fulfil. The result is always guilty self-absorption rather than rejoicing liberation. To call the Holy Spirit Gift reminds us that here we are not in the calculating world of benefits conferred in proportion to conditions fulfilled, but in the kingdom of a gracious Father who generously imparts his Spirit in free unconditional grace to people who do not and could not earn such a Gift, and in the same generosity opens and prepares them to receive it.

2. To describe the Holy Spirit as Gift emphasises that we are in the realm of dynamic relationships, the movement from a giver to a receiver, the opening up of one person to another. We are concerned with the impartation of life, truth, love and power from divine persons to human persons, with the self-giving of God to man that creates and evokes the responsive self-giving of man to God. The very notion of gift reminds us that the Holy Spirit cannot be studied in isolation, in and for himself. A gift is meaningless without a

giver and a receiver. So the word Spirit is a word that has meaning only in a relationship. The Spirit is, in Bishop John V. Taylor's suggestive phrase, 'the Go-Between God'. He is what he is and does what he does only within a network of divine and divine-human relationships.

It is therefore only from within that set of divine-human relationships that we call the Church that the Spirit can be identified and recognised, even although he works un-identified and unrecognised in all men and in all creation. There can be no theoretical academic knowledge of the Spirit. He can be met only where God's love is being poured out into people's hearts (Romans 5:5). The Pentecost of Acts 2 is not solitary ecstasy; it is corporate receptivity. In the New Testament the Spirit typically comes to groups of people together, not to individuals alone. Discussions of the so-called baptism in the Holy Spirit have often gone awry.[3] They have not taken account of that corporate dimension that is so evident in the New Testament from Pentecost on; they have failed to see that the coming of the Spirit takes place when people are together, and that it results in new relationships with God and with fellow Christians, not as a remote consequence but as the heart and centre of what the Spirit is doing.

These relationships are not set and static but dynamic and active. The three characteristically biblical symbols for the Spirit – wind (John 3:8), water (John 7:37-39), and fire (Matthew 3:11, Acts 2:3-4) – all point to a mysterious dynamic energy that destroys one kind of life and gives birth to another. It is only by involvement in these powerful dynamic relationships that we can know the Holy Spirit.

3. When we describe the Holy Spirit as Gift we are emphasising that we are in the personal realm. A gift is a gift in the proper sense only if it embodies the intention of a donor to give it and it is received as a gift only when the recipient acknowledges that intention. A cow does not give milk; she has it taken from her. When I give the cat her food, the fact that I act in goodwill and even affection towards her is a matter of small import as far as she is concerned. But when I give my wife some perfume, the fact that it is redolent

of me as well as of Chanel No 5 is what makes it precious to her. It is a gift made and received within a personal relationship and it has its value within that context. In the same way the Holy Spirit conveys and expresses God's love to God's people: that is why he is a Gift.

But in the case of the Holy Spirit, it is not only that a divine person gives and human persons receive, but the Gift is himself a person in a way that we shall have to discuss in detail later. When God in Christ gives us the Spirit, he gives us nothing less than himself. A gift is often an object that is passed from one hand to another. But here the Gift is a subject, living, acting, loving, sovereign and free.

That has not always been clear in the theology of the Christian West, particularly in the Augustinian strand that preferred to speak of the Holy Spirit as Gift. One of Augustine's ways of distinguishing the persons of the Trinity was to say that the Father was the Lover, the Son his Beloved and the Holy Spirit the Love between them. The problem with this analogy is that love is a relationship *between* persons and not itself another person, so that Augustine failed to do justice to the distinct personhood of the Holy Spirit. In the centuries that followed, the failure continued and there was an increasing tendency to understand the gift of God in terms of impersonal grace rather than in terms of a fully personal Spirit.

As a result, the Spirit came to be robbed of that sovereign freedom that is so characteristic of him in the New Testament (cf John 3:8). That is why we have described him in our title not simply as Gift but as Giving Gift. He is not just a passive Gift but himself an active Giver. What God gives us in him is less like a fortune to possess and spend and more like a friend to cultivate and love. His gifts do become our possessions, but as Heribert Mühlen points out,[4] Paul is careful to distinguish between the gifts which we are responsible for using and controlling (I Cor 14:32) and the Spirit who, as the sovereign distributor of these gifts, is not controlled or used by anyone but gives whatever he will to whomsoever he chooses (I Cor 12:11). In all this the Spirit retains his own personal identity. He is in us, but he never becomes part of us.

He gives with the greatest generosity, but he himself is never possessed. Our relationship with him is, as we shall soon see, quite different from our relationship with the Son and the Father, but in all his dealings with us he acts as a person whose freedom is always maintained and who eludes all our attempts at manipulation and possession. The value of this Gift is that the one who is given wills to be given, and he comes to us as one who has the divine willingness to give. He is the Giving Gift.

So even at this early stage we have identified, even if in a rather formal and abstract way, some of the defining characteristics of the Holy Spirit. His field of operation is dynamic personal relationships and we are to acknowledge him in the unconditional freedom of his divine grace.

The Holy Spirit and Mary

But if all this involves dynamic personal relationships, then it is to one of the most significant of these in all its particularity that we must now turn. The place at which, according to Matthew and Luke and the credal tradition of the Church, the Holy Spirit begins to reveal himself in his New Testament fulness is in relation to Mary the mother of Jesus.

Of course when the Creed brings the Holy Spirit and Mary together, the subject of the sentence is not either of them, but 'Jesus Christ, his only Son our Lord, who was conceived by the Holy Spirit and born of the virgin Mary'. If the Spirit works revealingly in Mary, it is not for her sake or yet for his own, but so that Jesus Christ can be formed in her and born from her. Mary's response is not to the Holy Spirit as such but to the promise about Jesus that is made to her (Luke 2:26–38). The christological concentration is central from the start and anything that we say about Mary and the Spirit that is not related to that centre will be literally eccentric and distorted.

Nevertheless, if the gospel as summarised in the creeds has a christological centre, it also has a mariological starting point. It is through Mary and no one else that Christ is born in a way that reveals both the nature and action of the Spirit and that constitutes and establishes the unique blessedness of Mary among women (Luke 1:42). Much modern post-Vatican 2 Catholic mariology has a scriptural and ecumenical character that the older mariology almost entirely lacked. It sees Mary not as the exalted queen of heaven distributing the gifts and graces of the Spirit, but as the model charismatic, the one in whom the Spirit began to do the work that would have its prototype and climax not in her but in her Son. What happened to her in Nazareth is not the completion of the New Testament work of the Spirit but its starting point. It is therefore right that in this introductory chapter she should have her place and her honour. In her we are shown what is on the way in Jesus, her son.

The accounts in Matthew and Luke of the virginal conception of Jesus without a human father have had a poor press recently both from theologians and from certain bishops. Fortunately I do not have to argue that question here, but can rest content with indicating my own position. As I see it, if we give the scriptural narratives the benefit of the doubt and accept them till they are proved unacceptable, and if we believe in the God of the biblical tradition who is Lord of outward physical events as much as of internal spiritual ones, there is no reason why we should not believe that Jesus was born, as Matthew and Luke say he was, by the creative action of the Holy Spirit upon Mary without the sexual intervention of a husband. That is the basis of my own believing and therefore of what follows. Those who think that the birth stories are more legend than history may nevertheless come to terms with what follows by seeing in the story of the Spirit's dealings with Mary a parable and anticipation of his dealings with all who believe in Christ.

Thus we can see how the Spirit enabled Mary to receive Christ in her unique way, which is a sign and promise of how through the same Spirit the same Christ will in a different way be formed in all Christians. Here we make contact with the understanding of Mary as the model charismatic common in post-Vatican 2 Catholicism and expounded in the context of the charismatic renewal by such writers as

René Laurentin and Cardinal L.J. Suenens in a way that is
easy for non-Roman Christians to assimilate.[5] As Cardinal
Suenens puts it: 'She is the Christian *par excellence*, filled to
overflowing with the Spirit of Christ ... Mary's role is not in
the order of obtaining grace. The Spirit alone is and remains
the Envoy of the Father and the Son. Her place is not as a
mediator. Mary's role is in relation to our response. In union
with her and following in her steps, we are helped to receive
the Holy Spirit and to listen to his promptings'.[6]

We may wonder if the picture of Mary as the well-nigh
perfect Christian implicit in that passage has scriptural
warrant and want to ask what exactly is the nature of our
'union' with her and of the 'help' in receiving the Spirit which
she provides. But we can agree wholeheartedly with the
Cardinal's central assertion that the significance of Mary is to
be found in the unique way in which Christ came to her
through the Spirit and in the response she made to that
coming. Mary is, indeed, the model charismatic precisely
because what the Spirit gave her was not primarily tongues or
prophecy but the gift of the Son. Mary in her situation was
the first to receive and respond to Christ in a way that is
exemplary for all Christians whom also the Spirit seeks to
unite with Christ. Therefore, in her we may find a
personalised promise and prospectus of the whole New
Testament work of the Spirit. By looking at what he did in
her, we can open up the issues ahead of us and prepare
ourselves to deal with them.

1. We may note first the implicitly trinitarian structure of
the gospel stories of the birth of Jesus. Of course, Matthew
and Luke are not working with any explicitly trinitarian view
of God and take no note of the pre-existence of the Son who
was born of Mary. Nevertheless, in the light of all that we
know about the work of the Spirit in the New Testament, and
the trinitarian doctrine of God which the New Testament
gospel implies and requires, the threefold structure of the
Lukan birth stories is highly significant. They speak of a
sovereign God in whose loving purpose and miraculous and
mysterious action this birth has its source and significance.
They speak of the one who is born as the Son of God, which

clearly means here not just the messianic fulfiller who springs from the house of David, but one who has a unique and mysterious relation to God because his Father is not Joseph who is of the line of David, but God himself. The term Son of God, which in the Judaism of the time usually meant messianic king, has in the birth of Jesus begun to mean someone who is, in a completely new and mysterious way, directly and immediately related to God.

Further, the word and will of the Father that bring this Son to birth through Mary have their execution through the Holy Spirit in a way we shall go on to examine. This child is conceived not by the action of any man, but by the action of the Holy Spirit. 'The Holy Spirit will come upon you and the power of the Most High will overshadow you' (Luke 1:35).

So, this is a story of a God who has a Son and a Spirit in intimate and mysterious, if still largely undefined, relationship to himself. The action into which Mary was drawn was the action of the Father, the Son and the Spirit. The context is clearly, if still implicitly, trinitarian. Right from the beginning with Mary, we are pointed towards that trinitarian understanding of God which the New Testament account of the work of the Spirit presupposes and requires.

2. There is from the beginning with Mary an interdependence between the work of the Spirit and the coming of the Son. The conception of Christ in the womb of Mary is made possible by the creative action of the Spirit, but the creative act of the Spirit in Mary has as its one end and aim the conception and incarnation of the Son. The Son is dependent for his humanity on the work of the Spirit, and the Spirit acts completely in the service of the Son. This *mutual* subordination of Son and Spirit to each other, whereby each acts in dependence on the other, is already indicated and suggested by what happens to Mary. One of our major concerns in this book will be to explore again how Spirit and Son are related both in the gospel itself and in the life of God which the gospel reveals to us. We shall discover again and again not only that the Son receives from the Spirit, as he did at his conception, but that also the Spirit acts only for the sake of the Son and to further the work of the Son, as he did

at his conception. We shall find reason to correct the onesided emphasis on the dependence of the Spirit on the Son which characterised my earlier book, *Reflected Glory*.[7] The birth stories themselves insist that the Son depends on the Spirit for his coming into the world, and that dependence continues throughout his earthly life and beyond.

3. The birth stories raise the question of the relationship of the work of the Spirit to Mary's response. What comes to her is on the one hand pure gift. She is highly favoured (Luke 1:28), because this gift is gratuitously bestowed upon her. But, on the other hand, the story speaks of her willing reception of this gift. '"I am the Lord's servant," Mary answered, "May it be to me as you have said"' (Luke 1:38). The mood of the verb expresses not reluctant compliance but willing eagerness, as if to say, 'Yes, yes, please let it happen as you have said.' The gift of the Spirit is in no sense imposed upon her but is gladly received by her.

The question is whether that willing receptivity is to be seen as itself part of the gift and work of the Spirit to and in Mary, or as an independent act having its origin in Mary herself. In the second case it is by the grace of God *and also* by the autonomous self-originated act of Mary in receiving that grace that Christ is formed in her. There is a strong strain in Catholic teaching that emphasises Mary's *fiat*, as though God had sought and she had given her permission for the Incarnation to happen through her, so that in her own way she would become co-originator of Christ and of the salvation that he brings. On such a view Christ comes out of the free consensus of the two autonomous decisions of God and Mary. This kind of mariology exhibits the same tendencies as arminian protestantism which, of course, does not mention Mary, but insists that the reception of Christ and his salvation depends not only on the grace of God but on the free autonomous decision of the believer to accept that grace.

We are, therefore, left asking the question: Is Mary's acceptance given *by* her *to* God or is it also, and more fundamentally, given *to* her *by* God? Cardinal Suenens, true to the tradition of Augustine, wants to say the latter. 'The faith with which Mary received the offer of God is itself a special act of the Spirit in her. He is the source of all faith. Mary's free and active collaboration was permeated and sustained by the Spirit who worked in her "both the will and the action" (Phil 2:13). She remained totally receptive to his action in the very moment of her free response. Mary does not take the initiative: it is the Spirit who invites her and gives her the grace of surrendering totally to him. God's sovereign freedom shines forth in Mary.'[8] In other words, God's Spirit creates and evokes her, and our, believing response to him. We must indeed answer *for* ourselves, but we do not and cannot answer *by* ourselves. The ability to respond freely to the promise of Christ's coming is the work of the Spirit in us. Throughout the book we shall be concerned both with the Spirit's relation to Christ, and also with his relation to us and our freedom.

4. The story of Mary presents the Spirit as the Lord and giver of life. 'The Holy Spirit shall come upon you' (Luke 1:35) refers not at all to an act of divine *begetting* like the amours of the gods of Olympus with mortal women, but to an act of divine re-*creation*, the model for which is in Genesis 1. As the Spirit of God hovered over the face of the deep at the first creation (Genesis 1:2), so the same Spirit with the same creative intent hovers over Mary at the start of the new creation. No Jewish father, not even Joseph of the house and lineage of David, could produce this new beginning out of himself: it takes a creative act of God. Mary stands for Israel; she is the daughter of Zion *par excellence*, but the tradition of Israel which she embodies has to receive its fulfilment not from within but from outside itself. The fulfilment of the old by the new does not emerge from the old by a process of immanent evolution. Rather the new is given to the old by an act of divine creativity worked upon it. Those who are born to be God's children are born 'not of natural descent, nor of human decision or a husband's will, but born of God' (John 1:13).

The story of the virgin birth makes us ask questions about the spontaneity and creativity of the Holy Spirit and how that is related to what goes before it. How is the work of the

Spirit in redemption continuous and how discontinuous with his work in creation? When we speak of the Spirit are we speaking of God's immanence in the natural order or of the breaking in of the supernatural order? Such questions will be with us all the way.

5. The Spirit is the creator of fellowship around the Son. The togetherness of Mary and Joseph consists in the guardianship of the one who has been entrusted to them, who is the bond of their marriage, although not its product. Elizabeth and Mary (Luke 1:39–45) find a new kinship in their motherhood of two children who are born as a result of two different divine interventions that correspond to the part that each child will play in the drama of redemption. Simeon and Anna (Luke 2:25–38) find fellowship with Mary in their discernment that the promises of God will have their long awaited fulfilment in her Son. The Holy Spirit creates from the first a fellowship centred on Jesus, each member of which is gifted to play a distinctive part in receiving and proclaiming Jesus. Mary has her own unique place near the centre of that fellowship, because she is what no one else could ever be, the *theotokos*, the mother of God. The Spirit is from the first the creator of *koinónia*, life-sharing togetherness. He is a community-speaking Spirit.

6. The action of the Spirit in Mary produces both prophecy and praise. When Mary is filled with the Spirit she begins to sing *Magnificat*, and she begins to contemplate all that God has done for her and 'to treasure it in her heart' (Luke 2:19,51). The Spirit in her is the Spirit of worship, prayer and contemplation, who enables her to discern and interpret what God is doing in her and around her. To receive this Spirit is to share the counsel of God and to respond in the praise of God. By him we receive what God has to give, by him we offer all we are to God. From first to last he is the Spirit of prayer. We must look at what that means for our praying.

7. What the Spirit does in Mary is the beginning of the future. The conception of Jesus does not carry its whole meaning in itself: it can be understood only in the context of what it leads to in the ministry, death and resurrection of

Jesus, in Pentecost and what lies beyond. In the Spirit Jesus who is the world's future is born into the world's present, the end of time appears in the middle of time, the last things start happening in history. Every coming of the Spirit is an eschatological act, because in it the ultimate future to which God is leading us invades, touches and transforms our temporal lives. The Spirit brings into time, first into the time of Mary and then into the time of all of us, Christ who has conquered death and is the *eschatos Adam*, the ultimate man (I Corinthians 15:45), who by the Spirit shares his humanity with us and begins to transform us into what God made us to be. The Spirit in Mary inaugurates the *eschaton* and we must ask what it means that he does that in us as well.

It is therefore legitimate to see in Mary a preliminary presentation of the whole New Testament work of the Holy Spirit. In her he is indeed the Giving Gift. He is given to her by the Father, and, by his work in her, he gives her God's Son to be her son also. In her story we have a first glimpse of what the Spirit is going to do in Jesus and of what through Jesus he is then going to do in us all.

Notes on Chapter One

(1) J.I. Packer, *Keep in Step with the Spirit*, Leicester, I.V.P., 1984.

(2) This is one of the main charges against Pentecostals made by F.D. Bruner in his important book, *A Theology of the Holy Spirit*, London, Hodder and Stoughton, 1970.

(3) In recent years I have found that the phrase 'baptism in the Spirit' is more confusing than enlightening and have tended to look for other language in which to say the same thing.

(4) Throughout this book I am much indebted to Heribert Mühlen's quite seminal work, *Der Heilige Geist als Person*, Münster, Verlag Aschendorff, 1963, which unfortunately has never been translated into English. The reference here is to page 7.

(5) cf René Laurentin *Catholic Pentecostalism*, English Translation, London, Darton, Longman and Todd, 1977, pp 192ff.

(6) Cardinal L.J. Suenens, *A New Pentecost?*, English Translation, London, Darton, Longman and Todd, 1975, pp 205-6.

(7) T.A. Smail, *Reflected Glory*, London, Hodder & Stoughton, 1975.

(8) L.J. Suenens, *op. cit.* p 200.

Chapter Two

The Person without a Face

Our title phrase is from the French theologian, Yves Congar.[1] It points to the elusiveness and anonymity of the Holy Spirit which are, as we shall see, among his defining characteristics, both in the New Testament and in subsequent Christian tradition. 'He will not draw attention to himself' is a clear implication if not an actual translation of John 16:13.

We know the Spirit, not because we have a face to face encounter with him, as we do with the Son and through him with the Father. Rather we begin to know the Spirit when we begin to realise that our ability to recognise and respond to Christ and his Father does not have its source in us but is given to us from outside ourselves. The Holy Spirit stands with us on our side of the encounter with the Father and Son and makes it possible for us to know and confess them.

When the encounter is actually taking place it is the Son and his Father who fill our awareness; it is from them that we receive and to them that we respond. It is only when we disengage from the immediacy of the encounter and, as it were, stand back and reflect on it, that we become aware of the hidden and mysterious action of the Spirit in making it all possible for us. The presence and work of the Spirit is an essential factor in the situation, because it could not happen without him. But he is there to concentrate all our attention on the Father and the Son and not to attract it to himself. We could not confess *Abba*, Father, or *Kurios*, Lord, apart from the Spirit, but it is *Abba* and *Kurios* rather than the Spirit that we confess.

It is therefore possible to be over interested in the Holy Spirit, in a way that grieves rather than honours him. If the Spirit is in effect saying, 'Look at them, not at me,' then to persist nevertheless in concentrating on him is to frustrate rather than promote what he wants to do in us. As Dr James Packer memorably puts it: 'When floodlighting is well done, the floodlights are so placed that you do not see them; you are not in fact supposed to see where the light is coming from; what you are meant to see is just the building on which the floodlights are trained... This perfectly illustrates the Spirit's new covenant role. He is, so to speak, the hidden floodlight shining on the Saviour.'[2]

So the comparative neglect of the doctrine of the Holy Spirit both in the New Testament and in the teaching of the early Church, to say nothing of later, is not to be thought of wholly as a failure, but as something that is rooted, at least to some extent, in the very nature of the case. The mission of the Spirit is to glorify the Son and we are most honouring the Spirit when our attention is most focussed on Christ. It is only later when we ask *how* we came to the knowledge of Christ and of the Father that we need to speak of the work of the Spirit and of the Spirit himself.

This is in line with a famous passage from Gregory of Nazianzus, the Church father and theologian of the fourth century: 'The Old Testament preached the Father openly and the Son more obscurely, while the New revealed the Son and hinted at the deity of the Spirit. Now the Spirit himself dwells among us and supplies us with a clear demonstration of himself. It was not right, while the deity of the Father was not yet acknowledged, plainly to proclaim the Son: nor when that of the Son was not yet received, to burden us further... with the Holy Spirit.'[3] In other words there is an inherent appropriateness in the fact that the doctrine of the Spirit has always lagged behind the doctrine of the Son right down to our own day.

It is so in the New Testament itself. In the passage just quoted Gregory Nazianzus says that the New Testament 'hinted at the deity of the Spirit'. His friend and contemporary, Basil of Caesarea, noted that nowhere in the

New Testament is the deity of the Holy Spirit explicitly affirmed by calling him *Theos*, God. Nevertheless, Gregory's hints are certainly there. The Spirit is frequently referred to as the Spirit of God and in II Corinthians 3:17 Paul applies the divine name, *Kurios* (Lord) to the Spirit, implying that he has the same title to it as the Son to whom it is regularly applied.

Further, as Wolfhart Pannenberg points out,[4] the identity of the Spirit with God is required by Paul's argument in I Corinthians 2:10-12: 'The Spirit searches all things, even the deep things of God. For who among men knows the thoughts of a man except the man's spirit within him? In the same way no-one knows the thoughts of God except the Spirit of God. We have not received the spirit of the world but the Spirit who is from God, that we may understand what God has freely given us'. Just as only a man's spirit who is identical with that man knows the ultimate truth about him, so only God's Spirit who is identical with God knows and so can impart the ultimate truth about God. If God's Spirit is not as identified with God as a man's spirit is with the man, then the analogy that sustains the argument collapses. The divinity of the Spirit is implied also in such a passage as Romans 8:11, which speaks of 'the Spirit of him who raised Jesus from the dead.' Throughout the New Testament resurrection is seen as wholly a work of God, so that here the Spirit is seen to be involved in a divine work and thus to be identified with God. So, even if a clear explicit statement is lacking, the New Testament makes it quite clear that when we are speaking of the Spirit we are speaking of God.

The Spirit as Distinct Divine Person

But none of these passages answers or even raises the question that is to be central to this chapter, Is the Holy Spirit a distinct, divine person? The doctrine of the Trinity is that God is one divine substance in three distinct persons. The passages we have quoted give good grounds for thinking of the Spirit as participating in the being of God; but, is there a

. New Testament basis for believing that the Holy Spirit is a third divine person in unity with, but also in distinction from the other two?

Before we can tackle that question, we must clarify it and ask first what in this context we mean by speaking of a person. To embark upon a history of that slippery term in trinitarian theology would take us far out of our way and maybe out of our depth as well! We can perhaps rest content with a preliminary working definition that will be clarified as we proceed: a divine person is one who reveals himself as the source and centre of the kind of actions and relationships that, by analogy with ordinary human experience, we recognise to be personal. That certainly begs all the questions; but, in a common sense kind of way, we all know roughly what it means and at least for the moment it will serve our purposes quite well.

To continue the process of clarification we must recognise that to say that the Holy Spirit is personal can mean two quite different things. It can mean: 'Does the Holy Spirit act in ways that are characteristic of a person rather than in ways that are characteristic of a thing?' Or it can mean: 'Is the Holy Spirit a third divine person, distinct from both Father and Son and related to each of them as one person is related to another?'

We may ask; 'Is the Holy Spirit just God acting personally?' or 'Is he a distinct person within the life of God?' To ask if the Spirit is personal is to ask about his relationship to us and whether he acts in us in a personal or an impersonal way; but, to ask if the Spirit is a person is to ask about his relationship to the Father and the Son and whether he is a third divine centre and source of personal action and response over against them.

There would be nothing inherently illogical in concluding that his action is personal but that he himself is not a person: as we shall see, some theologians do in fact hold that position. We could hold that the statement 'Christ relates himself to us by the Holy Spirit' just means 'Christ relates himself to us in a spiritual way.' In that case the action is thoroughly personal, because it is Christ who acts; however, it involves only one divine person, Christ, and not two, Christ and the Spirit. In other words, on this view Holy Spirit describes the *way* in which Christ acts, rather than another *person* acting alongside and in unity with him. The Spirit had ceased to be a third divine person and has become just the way in which the other two act. This theology would make us *bini*tarian, affirming only *two* persons in one God, rather than *trini*tarian, affirming three persons in one God. The distinctions may seem subtle, but they are very important not only for what follows, but for our whole understanding of the person of the Spirit.

So, we have to deal separately with two connected but distinct questions: 1. Is the action of the Spirit the action of a person? and 2. Is the person who acts distinct from or the same as the Father or the Son?

The second question is the main concern of this chapter. Yet we need to look at the first, if only briefly, because it has often been discussed very fully. We can answer on a New Testament basis with a resounding Yes. The actions attributed to the Holy Spirit are personal actions, the doings of a divine person. When we encounter the Spirit, we meet not an 'it' but a 'he', one who guides (John 16:13), restrains (Acts 16:6), distributes gifts as he wills (I Cor 12:11), can be grieved (Eph 4:30), to name just a few of the distinctively personal actions that are attributed him. To encounter the Spirit is like meeting another person distinct from myself, who indeed enters my experience, but has a life of his own outside my experience and beyond my control. I possess the gifts of the Spirit but I do not possess the Spirit who gives the gifts. He stands over against me in the autonomy and freedom that one person has over against another. He is the wind who blows where he wills in all the mystery of his divine freedom (John 3:8).

John emphasises this in his preference for the masculine noun, *paraklētos*, over against the neuter noun, *pneuma*, when speaking of the Spirit. When he does use *pneuma* he deliberately uses the personal pronoun *ekeinos*, alongside the neuter noun to underline the personality of the one of whom he is speaking (cf John 14:25, 16:13,14). Paul makes the same

Demonstrative

point in I Corinthians 12–14 by distinguishing between the gifts of the Spirit like tongues and prophecy that are within the responsibility and under the control of the person to whom they are given, and the Spirit himself who remains sovereign and under no human control in the way he distributes these gifts.

Heribert Mühlen points to the New Testament image of the Spirit as a seal (II Cor 1:21, Ephes 1:13) in this connection.[5] The Spirit acts on us in the same way that the seal acts on the wax, so that what is characteristic of him is impressed upon us. Although seal and wax bear the same significant shapes, they remain distinct and different from each other. In the same way, although the Spirit makes us like himself, he and we remain distinct, the one from the other.

Even when the New Testament speaks of the Spirit in impersonal images, the chief of which are wind, fire and water, the images are used dynamically to show that they are pointing to one who has the will and the power to control us rather than to something we ourselves can control. Throughout the varied images used the personal sovereignty of the Spirit in his relationship with us is affirmed and maintained. The one who gives himself to us is one who is and remains other than us and distinct from us.

The moral quality of his self-giving depends on that fact, just as the moral quality of my wife's love for me depends on the fact that she is a free and autonomous person who chooses to use that freedom in giving herself to me. The combination of otherness and self-giving defines the relationships of persons to each other, and just that combination marks the relationship of the Spirit to us. We, as human persons, receive the divine Spirit; but, he does not become human and we do not become divine. He gives himself to us and remains himself: we receive him and remain who we are. Our relationship to him is always a relation of persons and not a merging of spirits. Thus the Holy Spirit is a person distinct from us who in his own spontaneous and sovereign freedom gives himself to us. So, in his dealings with us, the Holy Spirit acts personally towards us: that is our

answer to the first question and it is in line with the witness of
the New Testament and the classical Christian tradition.

We turn now to our second question, which requires a
longer answer. Is the Spirit a distinct person from the Father
and the Son? When we call him the Spirit of God, do we
mean that he is a source and centre of personal action distinct
from God the Father, or simply that he is the personal God in
outgoing action towards his creation? When we call him the
Spirit of Christ, do we mean that he is another person who
acts in the name of Christ after he himself has departed, or
simply that he is none other than the ascended Christ acting
now in a spiritual and invisible way? In other words, is the
Spirit an extension of the divine personalities of the Father
and the Son, the means by which they extend their activity
into the created universe and into the lives of believers? In the
Old Testament, God's word (Ps 107:20), God's wisdom (Prov
8) and God's spirit (Ps 143:4,10) are seen in that way. Is the
Spirit still seen like that in the New Testament, or is he
beginning to be recognised as a distinct person in his own
right, over against the Father and the Son and having
personal relationships with them? Is there a third divine
person involved in the Father's dealing with the world
through his Son? If so, how can his actions be identified and
distinguished from those of the Father and the Son? What
indications of the Spirit as that distinct third person can we
find in the witness of the New Testament? How convincing is
the account of that distinct divine person that has been given
in the doctrinal tradition of the Church? These are the
questions before which we now stand. In the rest of this
chapter we shall be particularly concerned with the New
Testament material that is relevant to an answer to them.

When we turn to the New Testament and ask how it
distinguishes the Spirit from the Father, and more especially
from the Son, we shall find that there is no single or
unambiguously clear answer. The New Testament evidence,
at first glance at least, leaves room for several different ways
of understanding the Son-Spirit relationship. In contemporary theology there are in fact three competing
proposals about how that relationship should be interpreted,

all of which claim support from the New Testament data.

Two of these proposals are in the most literal sense reductionist. One of them holds that we do not need to speak about the person of the Son, because the Son is simply a man filled with the Spirit; the other holds that we do not need to speak about the person of the Spirit, because the Spirit is simply the presence and power in the world of the ascended Son. So, in one case, talk about the Son is to be reduced to talk about the Spirit and in the other case talk about the Spirit is to be reduced to talk about the Son. The third proposal, which is that of classical trinitarian theology, is, once more in the literal sense of the word, conservative, since it refuses to make either of these reductions and appeals to the New Testament in support of its claim that Son and Spirit are two co-ordinated but distinct divine persons. We must examine each of these proposals more closely.

Proposal 1. Son-language can be translated without loss into Spirit-language. To understand Jesus we do not need to regard him as the eternal Son of God, the second person of the Trinity, made flesh, but only as a man indwelt by the Spirit of God to the ultimate degree. This is the position explored and developed with great logic and consistency by the late G. W. H. Lampe in *God as Spirit*.[6] For Lampe, to ask about the relation of the person of the Son to the person of the Spirit is to raise a bogus question. The real question here is about how the presence of the Spirit in the man Jesus is to be related to the presence of the same Spirit in all other men. Since for Lampe, Spirit simply means the mode of God's presence and action within the created world, the question about the relation of the Father to the Spirit is reduced to the question about how God can be both transcendent over the world as Father and immanent within it as Spirit, the Son being simply the one in whom that immanence is greatest.

Thus classical trinitarianism is reduced to a dynamic form of unitarianism. God is not three distinct persons but one person endlessly and creatively active in the evolution of the world into the realisation of his purpose for it. In this way of looking at things, when the divine Son is removed from between them Father and Spirit collapse into each other and divine Trinity becomes divine Unity.

Lampe expresses this drastic revision of the Christian doctrine of God as follows: 'We should recognise, not that we experience the presence of Christ through the Spirit, but rather that when we speak of the presence of Christ and the indwelling of the Spirit, we are speaking of one and the same experience of God: God as Spirit who was revealed to men ... at a definite point in the history of man's creation in Jesus Christ ... We may, if we wish, call this contemporary indwelling divine presence Christ ... Yet this Christ is none other than the Spirit. The single reality for which these two terms stand is the one God in his relation to human persons.'[7]

Lampe goes on to argue that, if we insist that a continuing personal relationship with the risen Christ is a central and defining feature of Christian experience, we shall be forced to consign the Holy Spirit to a secondary and ill-defined role, and to impose on our experience a complicated structure that it does not require. Christian experience 'is not an experience of Christ being presented to us by and through another divine agency, but a single experience that can be described interchangeably in "Christ" terms or "Spirit" terms. The attempted distinction is artificial. It leaves us with an insoluble problem of trying to translate it into a real distinction, whether functional or ontological, between "Christ" and "Spirit": the "Christ" who is made present to us, and the "Spirit" through whom his presence is supposed to be mediated.'[8]

Some of us would want to reply that in our relationship to Christ the distinction between the Christ to whom we are related and the Spirit who brings about that relationship, far from being imposed or artificial, is at the very heart of the matter. A simplicity that removes from the relation either the real presence of the risen Lord or the gracious activity of the indwelling Spirit, is a heretical simplicity that distorts the data and that is therefore achieved at far too great a cost.

Furthermore, Lampe recognises that the New Testament writers, notably Paul and John, will not support him in his proposed conflation of Christ experience and Spirit experience. This is because they have lumbered themselves with the unnecessary affirmation of a continuing relationship with Jesus after his ascension, which, according to Lampe, nothing in their Christian experience required.

For Lampe Jesus has disappeared like all other good men into the mystery of eternity, where he dwells *incommunicado* as far as we are concerned. The exalted Lord of Ephesians who rules and acts in his Church as a head over a body (Eph 1:22), and gives gifts to his people (Eph 4:7-13), who in Romans intercedes for us at the right hand of God (Rom 8:34), who in Revelation walks amidst the churches and addresses them by his prophets (Rev 2-3), is gone without trace. All that the Pauline talk of being in Christ can be allowed to mean is that the divine Spirit who was once in him is now in us. We may become like him, but we cannot hold genuine living communication with him. 'It is no longer I that live but the Spirit of God who was once in Jesus who lives in me' (cf Gal 2:20).

The evangelical personal relationship with Christ and the catholic sense of his real presence in the eucharist are alike swept away in favour of a bare memorialism, where the remembrance of Jesus is used by the Spirit to stimulate us into trusting and hoping in God the way he did, but all without him. Lampe writes as if the amputation of relationship with the risen Christ from Christianity is only a minor intellectual adjustment that has no important consequences for the life of prayer and worship. He agrees that much prayer is in fact offered to Jesus but comments: 'Prayer to Christ seems to be so identical with prayer to God who was revealed in Christ that nothing is lost if the Christ to whom it was addressed is translated into "God who was in Christ." Once more it seems that Christian devotion does not require the concept of a continuing personal presence of a risen and ascended Jesus.'[9]

Against this proposal let us see the almost explicitly trinitarian understanding of prayer that is developing within the New Testament itself. 'Through him [Christ] we have access in one Spirit to the Father' (Eph 2:18). Christian prayer is indeed properly addressed to the Father, as I argued in *The Forgotten Father*[10]; it is offered in the Spirit and

through the Son, where 'through the Son' does not mean 'in
memory of the Son' but in the power of his actively
interceding and mediating presence by which the Father is
brought to us and we to him. To eliminate the living Christ
from our praying is to rob it of everything that makes it
distinctively Christian: it is not simplification of worship but
its termination.

From a slightly different point of view Professor C.F.D.
Moule also resists Lampe's attempted elimination of
relationship with the risen Christ from the New Testament
witness. 'I want to say not only that as a result of him [Jesus]
they experienced a new world: but that they experienced
Jesus himself as in a dimension transcending the human and
the temporal... It is not just that owing (somehow) to Jesus
they found new life: it is that they discovered in Jesus, alive
and present, a divine dimension such that he must always and
eternally have existed in it.'[11] That is in fact, as we shall see,
the basic presupposition of almost every New Testament
writer and the diversity of the ways in which they express it
only highlights the more their oneness of mind about what is
being expressed. Within this agreed framework the Spirit is
the means of our being related to Christ who is alive and
present but beyond the earthly sphere, rather than the
substitute or replacement for him.

Lampe's proposal is totally unacceptable, because it cuts
the heart out of the gospel by removing the living Jesus from
the experience of the Church. Jesus is not just the historically
first Spirit-filled man: he is the Lord to whom it is the chief
business of the Spirit to relate all the rest of us. It is not
merely that through him we are brought into a new
relationship to the Spirit, as Lampe maintains, but that
through the Spirit we are brought into a new relationship to
him. The Spirit does not lead us on from him but in to him.

*Proposal 2. The Spirit should be understood totally in
terms of Christ.* Here we are invited to regard the Spirit not as
a third trinitarian person with the Father and the Son but as
the mode of action of the risen and ascended Christ in the
Church and in the world. The one who acts when the Spirit
acts is none other than the risen Jesus. The word Spirit

functions as an adverb rather than a noun; it is a description of *how* Jesus acts after his physical body is withdrawn. To say that Jesus now acts through the Spirit is just to say that he now acts in a spiritual way. One of the chief modern protagonists of this view is the Dutch theologian, Hendrikus Berkhof, in his important book, *The Doctrine of the Holy Spirit*.[12]

Berkhof is very appreciative of Pentecostalism for its rediscovery of, and emphasis upon, God's empowering activity among his people. In Christ he does not only justify and sanctify, as classical Protestantism has taught, but he also endows the Church with gifts for mission. Berkhof insists that this empowering is not to be understood as an autonomous work of the Spirit over against the work of Christ in justifying and sanctifying; all three works are to be seen as having their source in the risen Lord. Berkhof quotes Käsemann with approval as saying 'The Spirit is the earthly presence of the exalted Lord' to which Berkhof adds on his own account: 'The Spirit is the new way of existence and action by Jesus Christ. Through his resurrection he becomes a person in action, continuing and making effective on a world-wide scale what he began in his earthly life.'[13]

Berkhof, like Lampe, will have nothing to do with the traditional differentiation of Christ and Spirit into two distinct persons. 'This position is untenable... if we face the fact that the Spirit in Scripture is not an autonomous substance, but a predicate to the substance God and the substance Christ. It describes the act and way of functioning of both.'[14] We cannot quite say that 'the Spirit is merely another name for the exalted Christ' since Christ is more than the sum of his activities towards us: 'The risen Lord transcends his own functioning as life-giving Spirit. He is eternally in the glory of the Father as the firstfruits of mankind, as the guarantee of our future, as the advocate of his Church. His life... is more than his function towards us. At the same time, however, we must say that the word "function" is too weak in this context. Christ's movement towards us is not a mere action, for his entrance into us is a special *modus essendi* [mode of being], the mode of immanence in which however he does not cease to remain transcendent as the exalted Lord.'[15] To simplify, the ascended Christ does more than work in us; to speak of the Spirit is to speak of the way in which Christ unites himself to us. Spirit is not the name of a divine person but a description of the way in which the risen Son indwells his Church. When Christ works by the Spirit, there are not two persons at work, Christ and Spirit, but only one, Christ.

C.F.D. Moule, whom we found so helpful against Lampe, is similarly inclined to a modalistic rather than a personal understanding of the Spirit, an understanding, that is, that sees the Spirit as *mode* or way of action by Christ rather than a person in his own right. 'When Spirit is the mode of God's presence in the hearts and minds of his people, then there is a good case for personal language. But this still does not force upon us a third eternal divine person (in the technical sense) within the unity'.[16] And again, 'Threefoldness is perhaps less vital to a Christian conception of God than the eternal twofoldness of Father and Son.'[17]

That last sentence distinguishes Moule and Berkhof on the one hand from Lampe on the other. They are not, like him, *uni*tarian but rather *bini*tarian in their understanding of God. At the heart of the gospel is the 'eternal twofoldness' of Father and Son; they hesitate to take the further step that would make them fully *trini*tarian by recognising the Spirit as a person with his own identity over against Christ and the Father, rather than being reduced to a mode of their activity in the Church.

Nor is this position as idiosyncratic and blatantly at odds with classical Christianity as that of Lampe. Eastern Orthodox theologians such as Vladimir Lossky[18] in our own day have often alleged against western Christianity in both its Catholic and Protestant forms that it is, except in the most formal sense, binitarian rather than trinitarian in emphasis. Although the Christian West has, of course, always professed a fully trinitarian doctrine of God, it has always found it hard to give a proper account of the person of the Holy Spirit. It has shown an inbuilt tendency to regard the Spirit as the relationship of mutual love between the Father and the Son, or as the relationship between the ascended Christ and the Church. In fact, in much Catholic thinking grace rather than the Holy Spirit has been seen as the gift of God to his people, so that, except in the context of the doctrine of the Trinity, and, with some very honourable exceptions, the Holy Spirit has not often been a central concern of western theologians.[19]

This allegation is supported by the fact that Berkhof can quote so trinitarian a theologian as Karl Barth to support his own binitarian position. He quotes Barth as saying that the Spirit 'is no other than the presence and action of Jesus Christ himself: his stretched out arm; he himself in the power of his resurrection'.[20] There are other more genuinely trinitarian strands in Barth's doctrine of the Spirit, yet in his later theology there is a growing tendency to regard the Spirit as simply the way in which the risen Christ goes on acting in the Church. This brings him very near in practice to Berkhof's binitarian position, even if he would have rejected it formally in the name of a fully trinitarian understanding of the being of God.

In his ambiguous unclarity about the person of the Spirit, Barth shows himself to be a typically western theologian in the line of Augustine. While Augustine was of course formally trinitarian, he often presented the Holy Spirit as the 'bond of love (*nexus amoris*)' between the Father and the Son, a relationship between two persons, rather than himself a person. If the Spirit in God is seen as a relationship between the Father and the Son, it is not surprising that in his work in the Church he should also be seen as a relationship between Christ and us. For all the complicated and highly technical attempts of medieval theologians to overcome that difficulty, the fact remains that a relationship between persons is not as such another person.[21] The result is that in traditional western theology, there is no decisively unambiguous answer as to whether and how the Spirit is to be regarded as a third centre and source of personal action either within the life of God or in relation to the Church and the world.

Against this ambiguity eastern Orthodox theologians have always most vigorously protested, insisting that the Spirit is not to be swallowed up in the action of the Son in this way,

for he shares an equal divinity and has a distinct personhood
of his own, by which he is distinguished both from the person
of the Father and the person of the Son. The same eastern
theologians insist that, far from being an abstruse point of
theology without practical consequences, the western failure
to affirm the person of the Spirit in theology is connected
with a western failure to honour the Spirit and his work in the
worship, life and mission of the Church. These are the issues
that are involved in the famous *Filioque* controversy between
East and West which requires a chapter of its own to explain
and expound.[22]

At this point I have to enter a word of personal confession!
In my earlier book *Reflected Glory*[23], in reaction to the
tendency in Pentecostalist teaching to cut loose the work of
the Spirit from the work of Christ, I also, in the best western
manner, insisted strongly on the subordination of the work
of the Spirit to the work of the Son, and showed that there is a
strong basis for such a position within the New Testament. It
could be argued that Berkhof and Moule are simply bringing
our teaching about the person of the Spirit into line with that
Christ-centred approach to the work of the Spirit. Why
should we not go the whole way in subordinating the Spirit to
the Son and finally dissolve the person of the Spirit into the
activity of the Son?

The Person of the Spirit – the New Testament Evidence

To answer that question we must turn to the New Testament
to see if it will really allow such an abbreviation in our
doctrine of God. Will we be able to say what the revelation of
God, to which the New Testament bears witness, requires us
to say about Christ and the Spirit, if we regard the Spirit
simply as a mode of activity of Jesus?

At the outset we need to recognise that these are not
questions that the New Testament authors were themselves
concerned about, so that the material that they provide for
answering them is implicit and indirect, coming to expression
as a by-product of their dealing with the quite different

questions that occupied their attention.

Furthermore, we have to recognise that there are different emphases in the different New Testament writers on this matter, and sometimes, indeed, within the work of one author. Sometimes we can detect a tendency to identify Christ and Spirit in a way that is consonant with Berkhof's position, and sometimes a contrary tendency at least to imply a personal differentiation between them. That of course still leaves open the possibility that the traditional trinitarian understanding will be able to hold together the unity and the differentiation between the two better than the binitarian position, in which the identity is maximised and the differentiation minimised or even eliminated altogether. However, before we reach any verdict we must consider in more detail the evidence of some of the main witnesses.

(a) Paul. It is not hard to find Pauline passages that seem *prima facie* to point to precisely that total identification of Christ and Spirit which Berkhof requires. For example in Romans 8:9–11 Paul speaks of being in Christ and being in the Spirit in a way that suggests that the two phrases are entirely interchangeable and identical in meaning. Furthermore in I Corinthians 15:45 the last Adam (*eschatos Adam*) is said to have become life-giving Spirit (*pneuma zoopoiun*). Spirit, in other words, is the mode in which he communicates his new risen life to others.

Commenting on this passage James Dunn writes: 'Immanent Christology is for Paul Pneumatology: in the believer's experience there is *no* distinction between Christ and Spirit. This does not mean of course that Paul makes no distinction between Christ and Spirit. But it does mean that later trinitarian dogma cannot really look to Paul for support at this point.

A theology that reckons seriously with the *egeneto* [became] of John 1:14 must reckon just as seriously with the *egeneto* of I Cor 15:45b'.[24] On this showing Dunn would have to be reckoned with Berkhof and Moule. To hold that the Spirit is the mode of action of the post-Easter Christ is, in the light of the text that he is expounding, a highly credible conclusion.

However, more recently, Dunn has reached a conclusion much more sympathetic to traditional trinitarianism: 'As far as Paul is concerned, there is what might be called *a "trinitarian" element in the believer's experience* [italics mine]. It is evident from Paul that the first Christians soon became aware that they stood in a dual relationship to God as Father and to Jesus as Lord. This relationship and awareness of it was attributed by them to the Holy Spirit (Rom 8:15ff, I Cor 12:3). That is to say, Christians became aware that they stood at the base of a triangular relationship – in the Spirit, in sonship to the Father, in service to the lord.'[25] Thus alongside texts in Paul that do not distinguish between Jesus and the Spirit Dunn draws our attention to texts that do, and as we examine the latter we shall see that they occur in confessional and doxological contexts, that is, where Christians are confessing their faith and praising their God.

For example in I Corinthians 12:3, which Dunn cites, the distinction between Jesus and the Spirit becomes clear because in the confession *Iésous kurios*, 'Jesus is Lord', it is Jesus who is confessed whereas the Spirit stands with the believers and enables them to make the confession. We do not confess the Spirit, but the Spirit empowers us to confess the Christ who is distinct both from us and from the Spirit. It would of course be going too far to suggest that Paul was thinking explicitly about anything like a distinction between two divine persons here. Nevertheless, what he says implies a distinction between Christ who is at one end of the confessional relationship and the Spirit who is at the other. The Spirit, of course, remains in the closest possible relationship to Christ but here distinguishes himself from him in an action that has Christ as its object and the Spirit as its enabling subject.

The Spirit performs the same function in relation to the confession, *Abba*, Father, in Romans 8:15ff and Galatians 4:6, where it is the Father who is confessed and the Spirit who is source and activator of that confession. In both cases we do not confess the Spirit, but the Spirit works within us so that we can confess *Kurios* and *Abba*. There is here a real distinction between the Father and the Son as the objects of the confession and the Spirit as the ultimate subject of the confession that points in a trinitarian rather than a merely binitarian direction.

In line with this in I Corinthians 12:5-6 the Spirit is seen as the one who works within the body of Christ sovereignly distributing his gifts to its members, whereas Christ is Lord over the body who is to be served by the right use of these gifts. So, in the familiar words of II Corinthians 13:14, the grace of the Lord Jesus Christ and the love of God are the things that are to be imparted, but the Holy Spirit is the one who effects the *koinonia*, the actual participation in that grace and love. The Spirit comes from the Father and the Son to our side of the relationship to enable us to receive them and the grace and love they are giving us.

It is significant that it is in his teaching about prayer in Romans 8 that Paul most clearly differentiates between the action of Christ and the action of the Spirit. He there describes two offerings of intercession that are made on behalf of the Church. The first takes place in heaven where the ascended Christ intercedes for his people at the right hand of God (8:34). The second takes place in the hearts of God's people where the Spirit comes to their aid in their inability to pray rightly for themselves and intercedes for them in perfect accord with God's will and in inarticulate groans that words cannot express (8:26-7). Christ prays for us from a highly exalted position above us, the Spirit prays the same prayer from a position deep within us. The fact that this contrast is probably quite undeliberate as far as Paul is concerned, serves only to show that he is giving expression to distinctions that were inherent in his experience of Christian worship rather than imposed upon it.

We may note in passing that Lampe can fit Romans 8:26-27 into his unitarian framework only by denying that it is the Spirit who prays to God for us. All Paul means, he says, is that the Spirit inspires us ourselves to pray.[26] This serves to eliminate the incipiently trinitarian thought of the Spirit praying to God from within us. It does so however at the expense of sacrificing the central point that the passage is making, that when we cannot pray for ourselves, we need to

rely on one, distinct from ourselves, who, at the depths of our
being, is doing on our behalf what we ourselves cannot do.
We shall explore the practical implications of this passage for
our own life of prayer later. For the moment it is sufficient to
note the clear distinction it makes between the intercession of
Christ and the intercession of the Spirit.

To sum up, it is far from accurate to claim Paul in support
of a merging of Son and Spirit into each other. On the
contrary, there are many Pauline passages that point to a real
distinction between them and that also resist the binitarian
reduction that Berkhof proposes. Furthermore, there is a
distinct tendency to see Christ as the one from whom we
receive and whom, in turn, we confess and the Spirit as the
one who works at our side of the relationship to open us up to
the reception and the confession of Christ. In II Corinthians
3:18, a central verse for Paul's understanding of the Spirit, we
are described as being changed into the likeness of Christ by
the Lord who is the Spirit.

(b) Matthew. A parallel and even more explicit contrast
between the one confessed and the enabler of the confession
may be found in Matthew 16:17, where Jesus, at Caesarea
Philippi with his disciples, responds to the confession that
Peter has just made. The object of that confession is Jesus
himself: 'You are the Christ, the Son of the living God' (v 16).
It is made in response to Jesus' own question 'Who do you
say I am?' (v 15). In the answer given Jesus discerns a divine
activity that is not Peter's own: 'Blessed are you, Simon son
of Jonah, for this was not revealed to you by man but by my
Father in heaven.'[27]

Here the work of opening Peter to the truth about Jesus is
attributed not to the Spirit, but to the Father in line with the
claim in Matthew 11:27 that 'No one knows the Son except
the Father.' There is, in fact, a tendency in Matthew and
John[28] to attribute to the Father activities that after
Pentecost will be attributed to the Holy Spirit. In Matthew it
is the Father who enables Peter to make a right confession of
Jesus whereas in Paul it is the Spirit. Our present point, as
against Berkhof, is that in neither case is it Jesus himself. In
relation to Jesus the answer that Peter gives to the question

that he is asked is Peter's own. It is not in any sense given to him by Jesus. Jesus receives the answer, Peter gives it. Peter answers *for* himself; it is his own answer that he gives. The integrity of his discipleship as a free following of Jesus requires that it should be so.

However, although he answers *for* himself, he does not answer *by* himself; although the answer is his, its ultimate source is not in him, in his own 'flesh and blood' but is given to him by 'my Father in heaven.' Jesus discerns in the answer he receives a divine hand at work in Peter which is not his own. There is an action of God at Peter's end of the confessional relationship which is not the action of Jesus. For Matthew it is the action of the Father who is distinct from Jesus, just as for Paul it is the action of the Spirit, who is also distinct from Jesus. But in neither case is it Jesus who enables his disciple to confess him. Matthew might be cited in support of a claim that it is the Father rather than the Spirit who opens us up to confess Jesus, but he cannot be cited in support of Berkhof's claim that it is Jesus. On the contrary, he shows us that the freedom and authenticity of the confession depends on the maintenance of the distinction between the person of Jesus who is confessed and the divine person who enables Peter to make the confession.

(c) Luke. In the writings of Luke the distinction between Son and Spirit is emphasised more strongly that anywhere else in the New Testament. In Luke's account of the conception of Jesus, it is the Son who is born, but it is by the action of the Spirit that he is formed in Mary's womb. In the baptism of Jesus, the implicitly trinitarian element is at its clearest. The Father gives the Spirit to the Son, a statement that makes no sense unless Father, Spirit and Son are in some sense three distinct entities, even if it is still not clear in this context to what extent the Spirit is being thought of in a fully personal way. The Spirit here is the Gift, the Father is Giver and the Son is the recipient of that Gift.

Apart from reading Jesus' quotation of Isaiah 61:1, 'The Spirit of the Lord is upon me,' in his sermon at Nazareth (4:17ff), Luke shows little interest in the participation of the Spirit in what Jesus did in Galilee. He portrays the ministry

as the work of the Son. At the Ascension, which is recorded
in both Luke and Acts, that work comes to an end and the
Son withdraws. His going is followed after a short interval by
the coming of the Spirit. In the gospel Jesus is at the centre of
the action and the Spirit is in the mysterious background. In
Acts it is Jesus who has withdrawn into mystery and the
Spirit who has moved into the spotlight, for it is he who is
leading and empowering the mission of the Church and the
work of Peter and Paul. For Luke, the coming of the Spirit is
not the return of Jesus but rather consequent upon the
departure of Jesus. Here Son and Spirit are two rather than
one.

It is, of course, important even in this Lukan context not to
exaggerate the very real distinction between Son and Spirit.
They are never separate or independent. In Acts it is Jesus
who pours out the Spirit (2:33). If at his baptism the Spirit is
the Gift given *to* Jesus, at Pentecost he is the Gift given *by*
Jesus. The Spirit comes from the Father *through* Jesus and
the whole purpose of his coming is to empower the disciples
in their witness to Jesus (Acts 1:8). In Acts 16:7 the Spirit is
described as 'the Spirit of Jesus', although what that means is
never explained. So, to sum up, the bond between Jesus and
the Spirit is always maintained even when, as here, the
distinction between them is most evident. Nevertheless, for
Luke, it is one thing to be filled with the Spirit on the day of
Pentecost but quite another to travel the Damascus road and
meet the risen and ascended Lord.

(d) John. Of all the New Testament writings it is in John
that the identity and distinctness of Son and Spirit become
subjects of conscious interest and reflection. Where other
New Testament approaches major either on the identity of
the two or upon their distinctness, John wants to hold both
together. For John the coming of the *parakletos* is the going
away of Jesus (16:7) – here he is nearest Luke – but in another
sense the coming of the Spirit is the coming again of Jesus
(14:8) – where he gets nearest the Pauline tendency to identify
the two. In the upper room discourses (Chapters 14–17) there
is a subtle interplay of the two themes of the identity and
distinctness of Son and Spirit in a manner that goes a

considerable distance in preparing the way for the fully-fledged trinitarian understanding that was to follow.

In John also we can find the same tendency we have noted in Paul to emphasise the distinctness of Son and Spirit in contexts that have to do with confession and prayer. In John 16:13-14 Jesus defines the ministry of the Spirit in relation to his own. 'He will guide you into all the truth. He will not speak on his own; he will speak only what he hears, and he will tell you what is yet to come. He will bring glory to me by taking what is mine and making it known to you. All that belongs to the Father is mine. That is why I said the Spirit will take from what is mine and make it known to you.'

In a very real sense this whole book is an exploration and exposition of all the riches that are implicit in these verses, and we shall return to them many times. For the moment however we should note, firstly, the interdependence between the work of the Son and the ministry of the Spirit that it affirms. On the one hand, the Spirit depends upon the Son for the content that he conveys to us: without the Son the Spirit would have nothing to convey, because he brings no content of his own. On the other hand, without the Spirit, what the Son has would be shut up in himself: it is the ministry of the Spirit to convey it to us and open us up to receive it. Each depends on the other.

This interdependence itself implies a duality of persons and functions. The content ('what is mine') that is to be conveyed belongs to Christ, whereas the work ('making it known') of conveying it belongs to the Spirit. For John there is no question of Spirit being just another name for Jesus at work in the experience of his disciples. The personal pronoun that John uses for the Spirit – the masculine, *autos*, 'he', used in apposition to a neuter noun, *pneuma*, 'Spirit' – makes that clear, as does the way in which Jesus refers to the Spirit as another, distinct from himself, throughout the passage. The key phrase is, 'He will bring me glory.' In Johannine theology, glory is that which one divine person gives to another. Neither Father nor Son glorifies himself, but each glorifies the other.[28] So here the Spirit brings the Son a glory that he does not have in himself, but that comes to him through the activity of the Spirit in his disciples.

Pannenberg sees the importance of this as a basis for later trinitarian thinking when he writes: 'Was not Jesus the recipient partner with regard to the glorification as it was granted to him in the exaltation of the crucified and resurrected Lord? And is he not the recipient partner in his glorification through his believer's confession? Is not the glorification something that happens to Jesus from outside himself? If this notion proves itself sound, then one can perhaps justify the step to the dogma of the Trinity in AD 381 that called the Holy Spirit the third person in God alongside the Father and the Son'.[29]

In other words, our confession and worship are not, according to John, the self-glorification of Jesus, any more than what happened at Caesarea Philippi was, according to Matthew, the self-confession of Jesus. He is worshipped and confessed, in Pannenberg's phrase, 'from outside himself', but the ultimate origin of these acts is not the human worshippers and confessors, but the Spirit in his distinctness from Jesus who is at work within them.

This has enormous implications for our appreciation of the genuinely creative way in which the Spirit works in the life, thought and worship of the Church and we shall be exploring that later. The important thing to notice at the moment is that this creative glorification of the Spirit by the Son, that is highly significant for John, is a dimension of things for which Berkhof's binitarian approach cannot find any room. For him it is Jesus himself who is acting when the Spirit works, so that he must be seen not as the recipient but rather as the promoter of the glory that comes to him from his people. 'He will glorify me' has to be translated into 'I will glorify myself'!

We must, of course, remember that John is aware not only of the personal distinctness and mutual interdependence of Son and Spirit, but also of their essential oneness. As we have already seen, in chapter 14 the coming of 'another Counsellor' (the word *allos*, another, meaning another of the same kind) is understood two verses later as itself a coming of Jesus, 'I will come to you' (v 18). Such is the oneness between them that the coming of the one involves the coming of the other. Nevertheless, that oneness is affirmed alongside the real personal distinction between the two that we have just been describing. John, like Paul, but much more systematically, knows how to affirm *both* the identity *and* the distinction of Son and Spirit.

In all this John is quite clearly not pointing in the direction of Berkhof and his binitarian reduction, still less in that of Lampe and his unitarian reduction. He points rather, as Pannenberg suggests, towards the later patristic formulations that uphold both the personal distinction and the identity by maintaining that Son and Spirit are two persons who share the one being of God. That formula can be seen to be firmly based on the experience of the first disciples, as John records it, that the *Kurios* whom they confess and worship and the *parakletos* who inspires that confession and worship are personally distinct and at the same time essentially one.

Thus, to sum up, we have looked at the New Testament evidence on the Son-Spirit relationship and seen that it refuses to be reduced either to the unitarian position of Lampe or the binitarian position of Berkhof. Neither Son nor Spirit can be reduced without remainder to the other. If some New Testament texts emphasise the identity between Son and Spirit, others, like Luke, tend to emphasise their distinctness; whereas Paul and John, the former less systematically, the latter more so, hold both emphases together.

All this shows that, when we are probing this relationship, we are probing both something that is complex and mysterious and also something integral to the saving action of God, as the New Testament presents it. The action of the Spirit is the action of a divine centre of personal activity, distinct from both Father and Son. He is a person who hides his face, because his work is not to draw attention to himself, but to open us up to Father and Son. He can come from them to us and he can bring us to them, because he is eternally one with them. This understanding of the Spirit is explicit in the Creeds, but it has been the purpose of this chapter to show that it has been implicit in the New Testament gospel from the start.

Notes on Chapter Two

(1) Yves Congar, *I Believe in the Holy Spirit*, English Translation, London, Geoffrey Chapman, 1983, Vol III, p 5.
(2) J.I. Packer, *Keep in Step with the Spirit*, Leicester, IVP, 1984, p 66.
(3) Gregory of Nazianzus, 'Fifth Theological Oration on the Holy Spirit,' para XXXVI, ET in *Nicene and Post-Nicene Fathers* (Second Series, Vol VII), Grand Rapids Michigan, Eerdmans, p 326.
(4) W. Pannenberg, *Jesus, God and Man*, English Translation, London, SCM Press, 1968, p 172.
(5) Heribert Mühlen, *op. cit.*, para 7.29, p 217.
(6) G.W.H. Lampe, *God as Spirit*, Oxford, Clarendon Press, 1977.
(7) G.W.H. Lampe, *ibid.* pp 117-8.
(8) G.W.H. Lampe, *ibid.* p 117.
(9) G.W.H. Lampe, *ibid.* p 166.
(10) Thomas A. Smail, *The Forgotten Father*, London, Hodder & Stoughton, i'80, pp 168ff.
(11) C.F.D. Moule, *The Origins of Christology*, Cambridge, C.U.P., 1977, p 138.
(12) Hendrikus Berkhof, *The Doctrine of the Holy Spirit*, London, Epworth Press, 1964.
(13) H. Berkhof, *ibid.* p 26-27.
(14) H. Berkhof, *ibid.* p 28.
(15) H. Berkhof, *ibid.* p 16.
(16) C.F.D. Moule, *The Holy Spirit*, London, Mowbrays, 1978, p 50.
(17) C.F.D. Moule, *ibid.* p 51.
(18) Vladimir Lossky, *In the Image and Likeness of God*, ET, U.S.A., St Vladimir's Seminary Press, 1972, chapter 4, pp 71-96. Cf also Kallistos Ware in *A History of Christian Doctrine* (ed. H. Cunliffe-Jones), Edinburgh, T. & T. Clark, 1978, p 211.
(19) This charge is documented and explained in the works of T.F. Torrance. e.g. *Theology in Reconciliation*, London, Geoffrey Chapman, 1975, pp 98-9.
(20) Karl Barth, *Church Dogmatics*, English Translation, Edinburgh, T. and T. Clark, 1968, IV. 2 p 300.
(21) For a reasonably accessible account of the development of western trinitarianism in the medieval period see E.J. Fortman, *Theological Resources - The Triune God*, London, Hutchinson, 1972, chapters nine to twelve.
(22) See chapter 5 below.

(23) Thomas A. Smail, *Reflected Glory*, London, Hodder & Stoughton, 1976.
(24) J.G.D. Dunn, 'I Corinthians 15:455, Last Adam, Life - Giving Spirit' in *Christ and Spirit in the New Testament*, ed. B. Lindars & S.S. Smalley, Cambridge, C.U.P., 1973, p 139.
(25) J.G.D. Dunn, *Jesus and the Spirit*, London, S.C.M. Press, 1975, p 326.
(26) G.W.H. Lampe, *op. cit.* p 88-9.
(27) cf John 6:43.
(28) John 8:54, 17:1,5.
(29) W. Pannenberg, *op. cit.* p 179.

Chapter Three
God's Gift to us in Christ: God's Gift to Christ in us

We have seen that in the New Testament there is first of all an undifferentiated speaking of Christ and the Spirit, almost as if the two were interchangeable, because experience of the one was found to involve experience of the other. But, as the first Christians came to reflect on what is involved in confessing and glorifying Christ and the Father, they began more and more to distinguish the Christ who is confessed from the Spirit who promotes and enables the confession.

Pannenberg argues[1] that an important factor in this was the waning of expectation of the imminent, second coming of Jesus – the *parousia*. As awareness of the absence of Christ grew, so awareness of the Spirit, who was more unambiguously present, became stronger and more significant. It was the Spirit who in the prolonged period of Christ's withdrawal, joined him and his people together and bridged the gap between heaven where Christ had ascended and earth where his people still lived and suffered. If, unlike Pannenberg, we think that Acts reflects with some fidelity the way the Christian community was thinking about these things in the period immediately after Pentecost, we can argue that it did not take the delay of the *parousia* to make the first Christians distinguish the Christ who had ascended forty days after Easter from the Spirit who had arrived in a new way ten days later. However, increasing awareness that the period before Christ's coming was liable to be long rather than short was likely to concentrate attention on the distinctive work of the Spirit during that period.

If Son and Spirit were increasingly seen as two distinct sources of personal initiative and action, we must go on to ask how these two are related to each other. If the New Testament provides a basis for thinking of the Spirit as a person other than the Son, although one in mind, will and being with him, we have to ask if it tells us enough to enable us to describe the person of the Spirit in a clear, consistent and systematic way.

In his book *The Incarnate Lord*[2] L. S. Thornton discussed this matter with some care, because he too was looking for a New Testament basis for a trinitarian understanding of God in which the Spirit is recognised as third person. In his view the New Testament evidence does clearly draw the required personal distinction between the Son and the Spirit. Even in Paul, where the identification seems closest, careful examination shows that he uses Christ language in one context and Spirit language in another. For Paul, says Thornton, both Christ and the Spirit indwell the Church, but they do so in different ways. Christ indwells his people as the 'content' of their new life, whereas the Spirit indwells them as the 'quickening agent' of the new life. We are to be conformed to the image of Christ rather than to the image of the Spirit (Rom 8:29). We are to 'put on' Christ (Rom 13:14), not the Spirit. 'The Spirit is never regarded as the content of the quickened life. He is the agent of revelation who brings the content of truth to the spirit of man... Through his instrumentality a variety of *charismata* are bestowed upon the members of the new community. He is the energising agent who produces these gifts.'

Thornton goes on to comment on Ephesians 3:14-17: 'In Ephesians the distinction between the indwelling of Christ and the indwelling of the Spirit is clearly marked in one sentence. The writer prays for his readers to the Father "that he will grant you according to the riches of his glory to be strengthened with power through his Spirit in the inner man, that Christ may dwell through faith in your hearts". This text exactly agrees with the distinction which has already been drawn out. The bestowal of the Spirit by the Father is to have the effect of strengthening the inner life. The Spirit is the quickening cause and the indwelling of Christ is the effect of this quickening'.[3]

In criticism of Thornton, A. W. Wainwright claims that his distinction between Christ as 'content' and Spirit as 'quickener' is far too rigid for Paul and imposes an alien systematisation upon the many variations of expression he uses.[4] In Thornton's defence it could be said that he is only making explicit distinctions that are in fact implicit in what Paul writes, and, especially if Paul wrote Ephesians, Thornton's appeal to the way Paul uses his language is much better founded than Wainwright allows.

My own criticism would be rather different. There is indeed a distinction between Son and Spirit in the New Testament including Paul, but the way Thornton expresses it does not do justice to it. To designate Christ as the 'content of the renewed life' is to make his function far too passive and impersonal. Christ is not some impersonal life-content who in passivity is transferred to us by the Spirit's activity. Rather it is he himself who actively and dynamically establishes and maintains his completely personal relationship with us. Thornton's language must be translated into much more dynamic and personal terms to make it clear that we are talking about a relationship of persons and not a transfer of contents.

Let us, therefore, start again from Thornton's valid and helpful insight that both Christ and the Spirit indwell us but in quite different ways. Christ indwells us, in that we live our renewed life in a relationship with him that constitutes and controls all that as Christians we are and do. We live his life, we die his death, we share his suffering and his victory. We pursue his mission by participating in his risen and renewed humanity and all his authority and his love. All this happens in the sovereign dynamism of his initiating and self-giving grace.

To describe our union with him the New Testament uses language that stresses in the strongest possible way the organic oneness of Christ and Christians. We can exist apart from him no more than the branches can exist apart from the vine (John 15), no more than the limbs and organs of the body can exist apart from the body (I Cor 12). As the branches are in the vine, as the organs are in the body, so are we in Christ. To be separated from him is disability, decay and death.

However, at the same time as they are insisting on our unity with him as emphatically as that, the New Testament writers know perfectly well that there is a vital difference between the relationship of branches to vine and member to body on the one hand and Christians to Christ on the other. Our closeness to and dependence upon him is as real and integral as these other two unions, but, unlike them, it is a closeness and dependence between persons, because this is a union of persons.

Thus the unity and oneness do not abolish the fact that in this kind of personal union each party retains his own distinct personhood over against the other. It makes no sense to exhort a branch of a vine growing in a vineyard to abide in its unity with the whole vine: it has no say in the matter and can do nothing else. It does make sense to exhort Christians to abide in Christ (John 15:4) and to promise them that Christ will abide in them. They and Christ do not have the enforced unity of impersonal components of a larger whole; but, the unity proper to persons who have knowingly and willingly given themselves to one another. They are one because that is what they have chosen to be, and their unity does not contradict but rather depends upon and issues from that mutual choice. Thus Paul can accuse the members of Christ's body in Corinth of disrupting its unity and can commend to them the way of love, that is of willing personal self-giving, as the means of finding and maintaining that unity.

What it means to be one with Christ and yet for him and us to retain our personal distinctness over against each other comes out most clearly not when Paul speaks in terms of the body and its members, which have a set of impersonal relationships, but in terms of husband and wife who have a fully personal one. This he does in Ephesians 5, where he uses the marriage relationship to illustrate and describe the relation between Christ and the Church. In marriage there is both a oneness and a 'two-ness' and Paul, quoting Genesis emphasises both. 'The two will become one flesh', (5:31) so that 'he who loves his wife loves himself' (5:28). Divorce is, therefore, a tearing apart of that unity, of that one life that marriage creates and expresses.

However, in order to be one in their love, husband and wife have to remain two distinct persons: it takes two to love. Their relationship is not one of impersonal amalgamation, like glueing a leg to a chair or dissolving powder in water. It is a unity that includes in itself one person who loves and is loved in return, and another person who is loved and loves in return. It is a unity that consists of two people who knowingly, willingly and with feeling go on giving themselves to each other. It is what Martin Buber called an I-Thou relationship in which each partner affirms, respects and indeed increases the distinct personhood of the other by the offering of his love.[5]

A marriage in which one partner ceases to honour and respect the integrity of the other as a person distinct from himself is a marriage whose unity is under threat. A love that wants to possess and absorb the one it loves is a false self-love. C. S. Lewis somewhere wrote: 'She lived only for others: you could tell who the others were by the haunted look on their faces'. When I love someone, she does not become me and I do not become her. That is indeed the last thing that either of us would want to happen. The personal otherness of the beloved is the thing that gives the self-giving of love its motivation and its meaning. In loving her I escape from myself and am able to give myself to someone who is not myself, but is in the closest and most intimate union with me. This is a unity of persons and in this respect quite unlike any unity of impersonal things.

So it is with Christ and us. Our unity with him does not abolish either his personal distinctness or ours, but in fact presupposes both. Paul is so intent on affirming our oneness with Christ that he can occasionally seem to deny the continuing distinctness, but never for more than a moment. For example in the familiar verse in Galatians he can say: 'I no longer live but Christ lives in me' (Gal 2:20). Yet the next sentence in the same verse immediately makes it clear that what Christ abolishes is the old rebellious self of my sinful independence. My distinct personhood continues into my new life in Christ, for he at once goes on: 'The life I live in the body I live by faith in the Son of God who loved me and gave himself for me.' The faith that I place in Christ is an attitude of trust by one person towards another, and the love that Christ shows me is the giving of one person to another. The unity is so real and great that it abolishes all independence or isolation from between the parties; however, it is from first to last a unity between two persons who willingly choose to give themselves to each other. Christ does not become me and I do not become Christ; we become one because of his love for me and my answering faith in him.

It is when we understand our unity with Christ in terms of this indescribably intimate personal relationship between him and us that we can begin to grasp the part of the Holy Spirit in it. The Holy Spirit is not the one to whom we relate but rather the one who makes the relating possible. It is Christ, and the Father through him, who relates himself to me and to whom I relate; it is the Holy Spirit who enables me to receive Christ and to give myself to him. The Holy Spirit is the bond of our union with Christ, the one who comes from his side of the relationship over to ours and enables us to receive and to respond.

It is Jesus who is confessed by Peter at Caesarea Philippi (Matt 16:15); yet it is the Spirit who is at work in Peter to open him up to make that confession. It is Jesus who is confessed as *Kurios*, Lord, in I Corinthians 12:3; it is 'by the Holy Spirit' that our confession of him can be made. It is Jesus who is conceived in and born of Mary; it is through the action of the Spirit that he can be so conceived and received by her. The Spirit as the one who comes and acts on our side of our personal relationship with Christ and the Father is an almost literal translation of John's favourite word for the Spirit, *paraklétos*, which means the one who is sent to stand with us, so that we can make a right answer and bear a right witness to Christ and his Father. We are united with Father and Son, as persons with persons, and it is the Spirit who gives us the openness of mind, the motivation of will and the responsiveness of heart that make that union possible from our side.

What we have been doing is taking Thornton's valid but rather abstract and impersonal distinction between the Son as the content of the new life and the Spirit as its quickening agent, and translating it into more personal terms that keep us closer to the biblical sources. The Son is the person who by his incarnation, death and resurrection initiates our new relationship with God and fashions a new humanity in which we are to share. The Spirit on the other hand is the person who enables us to accept what Christ gives us, so that we can make our own what he has done for us and can respond to his 'Yes' to us with our 'Yes' to him. There is a great deal more than that to be said about the relationship of Son and Spirit, and we shall go on to say it; however, for the moment, it is good to reflect on this basic distinction between the person to whom we relate and the person who enables our relating. It will help us to understand more fully some important aspects of the Spirit's work as the New Testament describes them.

1. The facelessness of the Spirit. It would be completely against the grain of his distinctive way of working if he were to seek to relate us to himself rather than to the Father and the Son. That is why there is a way of concentrating upon the Holy Spirit that is grieving to the Spirit, because he has come not to draw our attention to himself, but to forge our relationship to them. We know the Spirit by knowing the Father and the Son and by coming to see that that knowledge is not our own achievement but the Spirit's work in us and gift to us. We come into the power of the Spirit most healthily when we open ourselves through the word of Scripture to the full range of the promises of the Father and the Son.

The rightness of seeing the Spirit's work in that way is confirmed by Paul's approach in the first two chapters of I Corinthians. There the single aim of his ministry at Corinth is to proclaim Christ crucified: 'For I resolved to know nothing while I was with you, except Jesus Christ and him crucified' (2:2). He does not write like a second-blessing Pentecostalist who would have two aims, the conversion of his hearers to Christ and their baptism in the Holy Spirit. Paul is exclusively concerned that they should be related to Christ.

Yet he immediately goes on to recognise that this cannot happen without the action of the Holy Spirit. To know the meaning and power of Christ crucified, they have to be delivered from Jewish understandings of God's purpose in terms of power and Greek understandings in terms of wisdom, because to Jews the cross is a stumbling-block and to Greeks it is foolishness (1:22-23). But how can people come to see that the weakness of the cross is the supreme exercise of God's power and the foolishness of the cross the supreme expression of God's wisdom? Not by either eloquence or persuasive argument, but by a deep conversion of the basic presuppositions of our thinking and judging that will bring our thoughts into line with the thoughts of God. This inner conversion (or paradigm shift in our thinking, to use the modern jargon) is the work of the Spirit. 'We have not received the spirit of the world but the Spirit who is from God that we may understand what God has freely given us . . . The man without the Spirit does not accept the things that come from the Spirit of God, for they are foolishness to him, and he cannot understand them because they are spiritually discerned' (2:12,14).

Here, quite clearly, the Spirit comes into view not as another alongside Christ crucified whom also we have to know and relate to, but precisely as the one who works in us to do what we cannot do for ourselves, by delivering us from ways of thinking that would make us reject Christ and bringing us into new ways of thinking that enable us to receive him. In other words, we know the Spirit as the one who enables us to know Christ. The Spirit reveals himself not as a new object of our knowledge, but as the one who makes it possible for us to know and receive Christ crucified.

For this reason the primary way of understanding the Spirit throughout the Bible is as wind, air, breath, *ruach* in Hebrew, *pneuma* in Greek, which you cannot see or know directly but only by its effects. So we experience the Spirit not directly but indirectly as the one who makes what is realised in Christ and promised to us actual and effective on our side of the relationship. The love and power that the Spirit brings are not his own; they are the love and power of Christ and the Spirit's part is to bring them from him to us. The great service of the charismatic renewal in recent times has been to open us afresh to this work of the Spirit in beginning to make actual here and now in the Christian community all that Christ has won for it. It must not become a movement that seeks relationship with the Spirit in and for itself, because the Spirit's word to us is always, 'You know me, only as you seek them, you receive from me only as you are open to them; you are empowered by me only as you serve them.' A spirit who offers us experience of himself and his gifts as the central focus of our Christian lives is not the Holy Spirit of the New Testament.

2. *The two-fold work of the Spirit.* This work involves both a *receiving from* and a *giving to* the Son and the Father. Both these aspects are held together in John 16:14: 'He will bring glory to me by taking from what is mine and making it known to you.' The Holy Spirit brings over to our side of the relationship all that is there in Christ – the life, truth, holiness, love and authority that the Father has given to his incarnate, crucified and risen Son. We are at the receiving end of a great movement of divine giving, first from Father to Son, and then from Son to us. It is the work of the Holy Spirit to see that we receive what God so graciously gives. The Spirit is the Spirit of truth, love, power and holiness, not because these things have their source in him, but because he delivers these things to us. He acts within our relationship with Christ to make sure that what God gives us in his Son actually reaches us. He takes what is Christ's and makes it known and effective in us.

And there is more. If he works at the receiving end of that great movement of giving that begins with God and reaches us, he also works at the beginning of the answering movement in which, in response to their giving to us, we give ourselves to the Father and the Son. In him God gives and man receives; also in him man gives and God receives. He is the Spirit of faith, the Spirit of praise, the Spirit of prayer, who glorifies the Father through the Son by bringing his lost children back to his house, and whose final purpose is nothing less than the restoration of the whole creation, so that it may worship and glorify its Creator.

So, the function of the Spirit is both to complete the movement of God's grace to us and to begin the movement of our gratitude back to God. Christ gives himself to us and the Spirit makes possible our reception of what he gives. In the Spirit Christ himself in his created humanity is given a glory that does indeed result from his gift to us but is in a real sense our gift to him. On the one hand, the Spirit gives to us what we would not have apart from Christ; on the other, he also gives to Christ, again in Pannenberg's phrase 'from outside himself', a glory that he would not have apart from us. At the one end of the relational bridge that unites us to him is Christ and at the other end us, and the Spirit ensures that the traffic across that bridge flows in both directions, first from him to us and then from us to him.

This is the direction in which the New Testament's sometimes implicit, sometimes explicit distinction between Son and Spirit can be seen to point. Accepting that it is God that we meet in Christ and that it is God as Holy Spirit who works in us to bring about that meeting, we still have to ask why it is necessary to think of two distinct divine persons at work in the encounter, Christ who comes to us and the Spirit who enables us to receive him. Why cannot we even now follow Berkhof, admit the need for these two divine activities and ascribe them both to Christ? What is wrong with saying that it is Christ who comes to meet us and it is also Christ who enables us to meet him? This has a simplicity about it in contrast to the traditional insistence that Son and Spirit are two distinct persons who share the one divine being, which can seem very complicated and ambiguous by comparison.

We have already given a biblical answer to that question and tried to show that within the New Testament there is much more evidence for a personal distinction between Son and Spirit than Berkhof will allow. We now need to ask in a more theological way why it should matter whether we merge the person of the Spirit into the person of Christ, or see them as two indissolubly distinct personal expressions of the one divine being.

We may at once agree that for personal faith and salvation it does indeed make little difference, because our relationship to God does not depend upon the depth or correctness of our understanding of the doctrine of the Trinity. If it did, who then could be saved?

That said, mistakes in trinitarian theology are still of very real importance, because they can lead to a misunderstanding of our relationship with the triune God, so that vital aspects of that relationship are obscured or underplayed. My submission therefore is that it is important to take into account the personal distinction between Christ and Spirit towards which much of the New Testament evidence points, because it has important implications for our understanding of the relationship between God and Christians on the one hand, and for our understanding of the being and nature of God himself on the other. We shall concentrate on the former in this chapter and on the latter in due course. I propose to point to three aspects of our relationship with God in Christ and to show in each case why it is important to recognise the personal distinctness of the Son and the Spirit.

The Distinct Personhood of the Holy Spirit and Human Freedom

It is important to recognise the distinctness of Son and Spirit in order to affirm our *freedom* over against Christ. Our response to him is not something he imposes upon us from outside in an authoritarian way; it is rather something that we bring to him for ourselves and that he receives from us.

Once again this can be best expounded in terms of the exchange between Jesus and Peter at Caesarea Philippi as recounted in Matthew 16. It is important to recognise that the questioning of Peter about his verdict on Jesus comes not at the beginning but somewhere after the middle of their time together. He and the disciples have kept company with Jesus, have heard his words, seen his works, entered into daily close relationships with him so that the evidence on which to base a considered verdict is before them.

It is also important to see that Peter's verdict is not the only possible one, as the initial question and its answer shows. '"Who do people say the Son of Man is?" They replied, "Some say John the Baptist; others say Elijah; and still others, Jeremiah or one of the prophets"' (Matt 16:13-14). There is a christological pluralism, a multiplicity of contradictory estimates of Jesus right from the start, much the same as there is today. The next question quickly follows. '"But what about you", he asked, "Who do you say I am? Amidst all the possible verdicts upon me, for which are you prepared to take personal responsibility and stand by as your own?"' Jesus had to await an answer that really did come from Peter. There must be no dictation or imposition by Jesus, the answer must be Peter's own.

And yet, although Peter answers *for* himself, he does not answer *by* himself. When his answer comes Jesus acknowledges it not just as another in the possible range of human interpretations that our religious creativity can produce. Peter confesses Jesus not as just another in the long series of prophetic voices who have announced God's judgments and declared his promised purposes to his people, but rather as 'the Christ the Son of the living God' (v 16), as the one, that is, in whom all these judgments and promises will have their final fulfilment. It is an answer that comes from the heart of the tradition of Israel in which Peter has been nurtured and that has in it authentic elements of human thought and judgment. When Jesus hears it, he recognises in it also a divine revealing activity giving Peter insights into the truth about him that Peter could not have reached on his own. 'Blessed are you, Simon son of Jonah, for this was not revealed to you by man, but by my Father in heaven' (v 17).

Peter has answered *for* himself over against Jesus, but he has not answered *by* himself: his answer has been given to him by the activity of a divine person other than Jesus himself, here, pre-Pentecost, identified as the Father. But post-Pentecost more specifically identified as the Spirit. God is present in this situation in two different ways. He stands on one side of the relationship between Jesus and Peter as the one who is confessed, and on the other side as the one who makes the confession possible. Here, true to the pre-Pentecost position of the incident in the gospel story, the 'twoness' is seen in terms of Father and Son. However, when Paul and John later reflect in the light of Pentecost on how Christians come to confess Christ, the Father is seen to stand with the Son as the objects of our confession (Gal 4:6) and it is the Spirit who is seen to be working in us so that we can make the confession.

What the Caesarea Philippi story brings out so clearly is that the work which is done in us is distinct from the work of Christ. The verdict we give is *about* Jesus; it is based entirely on what he does and is. The verdict is not given *by* Jesus, but by the Spirit opening our eyes to the truth about him that we could not see for ourselves and giving us the will to confess him as Lord.

The freedom of a Christian to confess Christ is in the last resort dependent on the reality of the distinction between Jesus and the Spirit that we have been making. Jesus does not dictate or manipulate our response to him, he *receives* it. He presents his evidence and awaits our verdict just as he did with Peter. In relation to him we have a real freedom to answer *for* ourselves.

Because that answer does not have its ultimate source in us, but is given to us by the gracious activity of the Spirit working in us, it is an answer for which we are bound to show gratitude rather than one for which we can take credit. It is indeed our own answer, thought out by our minds and assented to by our wills and stated in a way that is authentic to our culture and our human situation, just as Peter's was. Yet, although it is ours, it is ours by gift: it is given to us by the Spirit who works on our side of the relationship with Jesus, and has access to our minds and wills, so that he can liberate them to do what we could not do by ourselves. 'No one can say "Jesus is Lord", except by the Holy Spirit' (I Cor 12:3).

In such a context we can affirm both the freedom of the response that we make to the Son and the priority of grace, because that response is the gift of the Spirit to us. We are free over against Jesus to make our own answer to him, an answer that is of critical importance for our right relationship with God, as the whole New Testament makes clear. At the same time our freedom to respond to Christ is not a natural freedom that has its origin in us or that is our own possession. It is a freedom that is given to us and maintained in us by the Spirit. 'Where the Spirit of the Lord is, there is freedom' (II Cor 3:17).

In saying this we have not, of course, explained the mystery of the relationship between God's grace and our freedom; we have elucidated it by seeing it in a trinitarian context and so suggesting that the mysterious relationship between grace and freedom is closely connected with the even more mysterious relationship between the Spirit and the Son. As we affirm the connection and the distinction between Son and Spirit, so also we shall be able to affirm the connection and the distinction between freedom and grace. This will perhaps become clearer if we approach it in a slightly different way.

To distinguish between the Son and the Spirit in the way we have been attempting enables us to avoid two extremes. We might describe the first as a christological heteronomy – that word meaning in this context the authoritarian imposition of truth upon a person from outside himself. If Jesus is both the asker of the christological question and the giver of the christological answer, it can begin to look as if what is required of us is simply submission to the external authority of his word, rather than the exercise of our own minds in freedom to bring to him an answer that is ours and not just his.

This is not a merely theoretical possibility. In modern times eastern Orthodox theologians have often alleged that there is a close connection between the western tendency to subordinate the Spirit to the Son, on the one hand, and the western tendency to authoritarianism on the other. The latter has a typically catholic form, 'The Church says' or 'The Pope says' and a typically Protestant form, 'The Bible says.' In one form the living tradition of the Church and in the other the written tradition of the Bible, both with the person of Christ at their head, are in danger of being regarded as external authorities demanding submission and leaving little room for Christians to see and think through for themselves the truth and reality of what they profess. The biblical Christ who respects human integrity and seeks and awaits the free response of those who have eyes to see and ears to hear is in danger of becoming the dictatorial Christ who demands that we assent to fixed orthodoxies and sign the approved credal formulae on the dotted line.

As Vladimir Lossky puts it, this concentration on an authoritarian Christ and our union in faith with him rather than on the liberating Spirit 'raises again the question of the place of human persons in this union: either they would be annihilated in being united to the person of Christ or the person of Christ would be imposed upon them from without. In this latter case grace would be conceived as external in relation to freedom, instead of being its inner flowering. But it is in this freedom that we acknowledge the deity of the Son, made manifest to our understanding through the Holy Spirit dwelling within us'.[6] If that happens, the importance of what Christ is and does outside and apart from us has been onesidedly overemphasised at the expense of what the Spirit does within us and as a result our freedom has been suppressed by his authority. He has provided a confession for us rather than make room for us to answer for ourselves. A Jesus who does that is not the Jesus of Matthew 16, who asked: 'Who do *you* say that I am?' A christological heteronomy of that kind leaves no room for the spontaneity of what the Spirit does in the believer.

At the opposite extreme from heteronomy is *autonomy*, which in this context means that the source of authority is located not externally in Christ but internally in ourselves. It is not now that he imposes his truth on us, but rather that we impose our truth on him. Many contemporary radical approaches to christology are of this autonomous kind. They are less interested in discovering who Christ is in himself or in his relation to the Father and much more interested in what he is to us, his relevance to us and his meaning in relation to the way we think of ourselves and our needs. Since he can mean many different things to many different people, there can be many equally valid christologies of this kind and, within their own terms of reference, no way and indeed no need to decide which is nearest to the biblical truth about Jesus. There can be as many understandings of Jesus as there are types of human culture and each in its autonomy will claim the right to conform Christ to itself and make him whatever is most meaningful to it.

In this sort of approach I do not just respond to him *for* myself, which is entirely legitimate and, in the light of what we have been saying quite necessary, but I respond *by* myself so that my experience and needs control that response rather than the given facts of the gospel. If, for example, my way of thinking does not allow for miracles and a bodily resurrection, even if these are on almost every page of the gospel story, I simply discount them as first century myths that are meaningless to autonomous twentieth century man.

What happens here is exactly the opposite of what happens under the influence of heteronomous authoritarianism. There the work of the Spirit is discounted in favour of the work of Christ. Here the Spirit of Christ has been identified with our own spiritual awareness. The seat of authority has moved from Christ to us. Spirit is now another name for the religious activity of the believer himself.

If heteronomous authoritarianism is the danger that threatens much evangelical and catholic orthodoxy, autonomous subjectivism is at the root of many of the liberal and radical approaches that are much in vogue at present. It can even infect the charismatic renewal if the renewed Christian and his experiences are allowed to become the main focus of attention rather than Christ and his gospel.

Such an overemphasis on the autonomous freedom of the believer who confesses is just as alien to the New Testament as is an overemphasis on the heteronomous authority of the Christ who is confessed. Once more in terms of Matthew 16, it is not our 'flesh and blood', our autonomous human perceptions and judgments, that are the decisive factor in how we relate to Christ. On the contrary, the Father through the Spirit as a distinct divine factor in the situation has to act upon our humanity before we can rightly relate to Christ at all. Only by the Holy Spirit can we say that Jesus is Lord (I Cor 12:3). No one can grasp the things of God without the Spirit of God (I Cor 2:11). We have to be born again of the Spirit before we can see or enter the kingdom of God (John 3:3,5).

These are just some of the ways in which the New Testament makes it clear that our freedom to respond to Christ is not our natural possession but a gift that comes to us through the activity in us of one who is distinct from us, who has what we do not have, and from whom we have to receive. The Holy Spirit is not our spirit, although he works in us, but the Spirit of Christ and the Spirit of God. We are not the creators of the truth we confess. To confess Christ does not mean to conform him to our way of seeing things, it means to see him as he sees himself, and to let him show us who he is and what he will do for us. The Holy Spirit, just because he is the Spirit of Christ and the Spirit of God, shows us Christ as he is to himself and most of all as he is to the Father, because no one really knows the Son except the Father and those to whom he reveals him by the Spirit (cf Matt 11:27).

Jesus is not Lord because we acknowledge him to be so: the throne that he occupies is not one that we have built: 'God exalted him to the highest place and gave him the name that is above every name' (Phil 2:9). That is where he stands with God, and that is what the Spirit of God comes to us to show us. That truth cannot be changed in order to conform to our ideas: it is rather we and our ideas who have to be changed in order to conform to the truth.

To sum up, the truth as it is in Christ in its relationship to us is neither heteronomous nor autonomous. It is not imposed upon us from outside, nor is it created by us from inside. It stands in its own right apart from us, but the Holy Spirit comes so that we may see it for ourselves, grasp it with our own minds and affirm it freely with our own wills. We are not its source but it is given to us, really and authentically given, so that with joy and understanding we may embrace and confess it.

The Holy Spirit is not to be displaced by Christ, because

that would lead to heteronomy; neither is he to be displaced by our spirits, because that would lead to autonomy. He is distinct both from Jesus and from us and we can understand our Christian freedom rightly only in the light of his distinctness. Our response to Christ in the Spirit is a free response, not one that is imposed or dictated. That response is given by us to him and not by him to us. We respond *for* ourselves. But at the same time the response is given to us, not by Christ, but by the Spirit acting on our side of the relationship that we have with Christ. When we freely confess Christ and his Father, it is because there takes place in us a divine activity that is not the activity of the divine persons we confess, but the activity of the Spirit, the divine person who liberates us for the confession.

Our confession of Christ is a true confession, because the Spirit who enables us to make it is of one being with Christ and therefore can bring the truth from him to us. At the same time our confession to Christ is a free confession that we bring to Christ for ourselves, because the Spirit who enables us to make it is in his person distinct from Christ. Thus the New Testament freedom to respond to Christ *for* ourselves – rejecting heteronomy – but not *by* ourselves – rejecting autonomy – is best understood in the context of a fully trinitarian understanding of God, in which the Spirit is recognised as a person distinct from the Son. We are free only if the Spirit makes us free to confess the Son.

The Distinct Personhood of the Holy Spirit and his Continuing Creativity

It is important to recognise the distinctness of Son and Spirit in order to affirm the *creativity* of the Spirit in relation to Jesus. We shall understand this better if we explore the (at first sight) rather startling statement that from one point of view Jesus is quite final for Christians, but from another point of view he is not.

Jesus is final in the sense that he is the one true and living way by which we come to the Father (John 14:6). His is the one name given among men by which we can be saved (Acts 4:12). He is the one incarnate Word of God who will never be replaced by any other (John 1:14). He bears the name *kurios*, Lord, which is the name above every name which every tongue must confess and at which every knee must bow (Phil 2:9–11).

The Holy Spirit, therefore, in all his works and ways comes from Jesus and witnesses to Jesus. To do that is indeed the defining characteristic of the Holy Spirit, as I John 4:2–3 makes clear. 'This is how you can recognise the Spirit of God: Every spirit that acknowledges that Jesus Christ has come in the flesh is from God, but every spirit that does not acknowledge Jesus is not from God.' The Holy Spirit is from start to finish the Spirit of Christ, and he brings no revelation or way of salvation that is different from or additional to the one normative revelation and salvation of God in Christ. 'All that belongs to the Father is mine. That is why I said that the Spirit will take from what is mine and make it known to you' (John 16:15). Everything that the Spirit does is implicitly included in that word. In that sense the Son of God is final both for us and for the Spirit who witnesses to him in us, and to abolish that finality in order to make room for other revelations, other salvations, other religions is in the end of the day to rob us of our gospel.

But Jesus is *not* final in the other sense that his words and deeds in the short years of his earthly life and ministry are the total and exhaustive explication of all that he is. If that were so, the whole work of the Church in every generation could only be to repeat what Jesus said and re-enact what Jesus did on his way from Nazareth to Calvary. We would then be committed to saying and doing only what could find explicit warrant in the words and deeds of Jesus as recorded in the gospel narratives or in the words and deeds of the apostles who were most closely connected with him and immediately authorised by him, as they are recorded in the rest of the New Testament.

That, put as simply as it can be, is the classical Protestant position (at least in its Calvinist form) which therefore tends, in its understanding of the Holy Spirit, to lay all the emphasis

Propositional

upon his work of guaranteeing and authenticating the Scriptures and, by so doing, to bind us exclusively to the teaching and practices that Scripture explicitly authorises. The young Calvin, for example, had great difficulty in accepting the doctrine of the Trinity precisely because it did not have this explicit scriptural warrant and was not expressed in the language of the biblical texts.

Any view that restricts the Spirit to authenticating and enforcing what is written in Scripture is quite inadequate in the light of Jesus' own promises about the creative action of the Spirit in the Church. Everything that the Spirit does is, of course, related to and continuous with what was said and done by the earthly Jesus and with what was written by his apostles. Nothing the Spirit says or does can ever contradict what Jesus said and did. His consistency and continuity with Jesus are his defining and identifying characteristics. He will continually bring to our remembrance all that Jesus said, did and was (John 14:26), as we have just been saying. He will indeed go on enlivening the written word of Scripture to us, so that it will for ever be received and believed in the Church.

However, that is not all he will do. Although the Spirit will always bear witness to the Son incarnate in Jesus, and to none other than him, he will expose, explicate, interpret and apply the truth as it is in Christ in a way that is faithful to its first biblical exposition but that goes far beyond it and relates the same truth to questions and situations that are quite different from any Jesus or the apostles encountered and dealt with. If we are to take the gospels and especially John's gospel seriously, Jesus himself seems to have had a clear sense that through the ministry of the Holy Spirit the saving moment of God's grace, of which he himself was the one source and centre, would go far beyond where he himself had taken it in his days on earth.

When brought before hostile rulers and authorities his disciples would not simply quote and repeat what he had said, but would be given by the Spirit new words that Jesus had not spoken that would penetrate deep into a new situation and bring the truth of Jesus to bear upon it (Luke 12:12, cf Mark 13:11). Such a looking forward to what the

Spirit would do in the future that would go beyond what Jesus is doing in the present is a marked feature of the upper room discourses in John 14-16. The disciples, when the Paraclete has come to them, will not only repeat the works of Jesus but will go on to do ever greater works (John 14:12). When the Spirit comes he will lead them into an understanding of the relationship of the Father and the Son and of both to themselves which is far beyond anything they have at the moment (14:20-21).

The Counsellor will do for the world what Jesus has not done – convince it of sin and righteousness and judgment (16:8). Jesus himself has not delivered to them all the truth they need to hear, because they are not yet able to bear it. He has 'much more to say to you,' (16:12) and it will be the Spirit who will guide them into all this new truth. The Spirit will certainly not originate or contribute any novel truth of his own. 'He will not speak on his own, he will speak only what he hears' (16:13). Nevertheless, on that basis he will prepare the disciples for things to come in a way that Jesus has not. As Raymond Brown remarks in his commentary on the passage: 'The declaration of the things to come consists in interpreting in relation to each coming generation the contemporary significance of what Jesus has said and done. The best Christian preparation for what is coming to pass is not an exact foreknowledge of the future but a deep understanding of what Jesus means for one's own time'.[7]

All this Johannine evidence points clearly towards two firm conclusions. On the one hand the activity of the Spirit remains in the closest possible co-ordination with the activity of Christ. On the other hand, in new contexts and in response to new challenges to it, the Spirit explicates the truth of Christ in a way that none of the first apostolic witnesses could ever have contemplated. To the perennial question, 'Who do you say that I am?', the Spirit has throughout Christian history produced a whole series of explicating answers that bring out in ever new ways the universal and cosmic significance of the Messiah of Israel for all human cultures in every land and in every century. He does not just repeat the biblical confession; he brings into the open the hidden depths of truth that they contain.

One of the limitations of the mirror language of II Corinthians 3:18, on which I based the title and the central content of my book, *Reflected Glory*, is that it fails to express the creativity of the Spirit on which we have just been insisting. It is not adequate to think of the Spirit as the light that proceeds from Christ and enables him to be reflected as in a mirror in the lives of Christians. On this analogy, light simply transmits to the mirror the object that it reflects, whereas the Spirit does more than that in relation to Christ.

It would be more in line with the Johannine understanding of the work of the Spirit in relation to the Son, to think of the Spirit much more personally and creatively as an artist whose one subject is the Son, and who is concerned to paint countless portraits of that subject on countless human canvases using the paints and brushes provided by countless human cultures and historical situations. On such an analogy the christological centre is fully affirmed and maintained. It is Jesus, the incarnate Son of the Father, and no other that the Spirit seeks to portray. Each portrait is successful and creative, not because it makes of him what he is not, by forming him in our likeness and conforming him to our preferences and predilections, but because it uses ever new cultural approaches and historical situations to bring out more of the infinite variety of saving truth that is in him.

No one portrayal can ever capture such a subject completely. But in them all Jesus is the model; the Spirit is the artist who is totally dedicated to do justice to that model and who has such unity of being with the model that he knows him through and through. Christian churches and people, sharing the concerns, the language, the questions, the achievements and the sufferings of the lands and times in which they live, are the raw materials that he uses to fashion ever new portraits of Jesus. They will all show him in his basic self-identity and continuity, but they will all make explicit something that was implicit from the first but that now the

divine artist highlights and offers to our faith and love with
new clarity and emphasis.

The gospel of John can itself be seen as among the first in a
series of portraits of Jesus that do not simply repeat his story
in its original setting, but explore it so as to bring out in a
fresh way its meaning and significance for people different
from those to whom it was originally addressed. Jesus lived
as a Jew among Jews; John makes him accessible to the
Greek world in a way that illuminates his universal Lordship
by showing what he will always be to all men. It is the first of
many masterpieces in which the creative hand of the divine
artist, the Holy Spirit, can be discerned by those who have
eyes to see.

One of the limitations of some brands of Protestant
evangelicalism is that they tend to emphasise the finality of
Jesus and the scriptural witness to him in a way that
depreciates the creativity of the Holy Spirit. The New
Testament Scriptures are seen not simply as the *primary*
witnesses to Christ, as indeed they are, but as the *final*
witnesses which have simply to be repeated in different words
by all subsequent preaching and theology.

There are modern charismatic versions of this as well as the
classical Protestant ones. The notion of 'restoration' much
beloved of the so-called house churches is often seen as a
matter of stripping away the useless and indeed harmful
accretions that have adhered to the gospel over the decadent
and unspiritual Christian centuries so as to restore to us the
faith and practice of the first century church in all their
pristine purity. Dogma, liturgy, church order are all
dismissed as the worthless traditions of men that have
entrapped and largely nullified the grace and truth of God.
We are bidden to get back to the beginning, to say it as they
said it then, and do it as they did it then. We are to bring back
the kind of worship Paul describes in I Corinthians 14 and, at
our celebrations of the Lord's Supper, do exactly and only
what we think Jesus did in the upper room on the night he
was betrayed. If there is no explicit statement that the
apostolic churches baptised anyone but believing adult
converts, that settles the matter and we must do the same.

(margin note: why KS loveh? love? creative)

In other words, if we cannot find a Bible verse for it, we should not believe it or do it. The reason why many evangelicals in the mainline churches are embarrassed about how to meet the criticisms of the house churches, is that they share the basic presupposition on which these criticisms are based – that Christian belief and practice is finally and permanently fixed by the teaching and practice recorded in the New Testament Scriptures.

All this can amount to a denial of the creativity of the Holy Spirit in the post-biblical tradition of the Church. A very proper protest at the Reformation against traditions of faith and practice that were in blatant contradiction to the scriptural gospel, has been turned into a wholesale rejection of tradition in favour of Scripture. It is certainly true that not everything that has been taught and done in the history of the Church has been a work of the Holy Spirit. Tradition does need to be approached warily and critically – that was the necessary and helpful Protestant warning that we need to go on heeding. However, if it is indeed true that not all tradition has its source in the Holy Spirit, it is equally true that much of it does. The Holy Spirit has given to the Church down the centuries much that is not given in Scripture, although it is in agreement with Scripture.

For example, the doctrine of God as Trinity, as Calvin realised, and the christology of the Council of Chalcedon with its claim that Christ is true God and true man in one undivided person, can neither of them be found explicitly in the New Testament in the sense that you can establish them from biblical proof texts. They represent the still implicit and largely tacit presuppositions within which the New Testament writers speak of God and of Jesus. It was the Church, in its struggles with heretical alternatives, that was led in the creativity of the Spirit to make them explicit in the doctrines of the creeds.

To put the same thing another way: they are biblical doctrines, not in the sense that they are clearly formulated in the Bible, but in the sense that they are the framework within which the biblical message can be best expressed. Only if God is Father, Son and Holy Spirit, only if Jesus is true God and true man in one person can we say what the New Testament says about God's saving action in his person and work.

These doctrines are the answers given by the Holy Spirit in a whole series of fresh historical situations to the question of Jesus, 'Who do you say that I am?' They are not simply repetitions of the biblical answers to that question, but legitimate developments and explications of them. They do not replace or even add to the biblical answers, but simply unfold the meaning of these answers in critical confrontations between God's truth and distorting errors in situations that the biblical authors could never have contemplated.

To ask whether a doctrine is biblical is not the same as to ask whether it can be supported by a compilation of biblical texts. It is to raise the much more subtle question whether it is in real continuity and agreement with the gospel to which Scripture bears witness. To give an answer will require biblical knowledge and theological expertise, but much more it will require spiritual discernment. When we hear fresh contemporary answers to the questions about himself and his work posed by Jesus, we have to ask whether we are dealing simply with the reaction of flesh and blood turning the truth into a lie, or with the interpreting activity of the Holy Spirit leading us, as Jesus promised, into new dimensions of the truth – or even perhaps with a mixture of both.

Sometimes in doctrinal debate among Christians a temporary impasse can be reached, because what one side takes to be a new discernment of the truth given by the Spirit, the other side sees as the distorting activity of the flesh with its engrained false starting points and sinful prejudices. In such a situation nothing is solved by quoting texts and shouting. 'The Bible says' at one another; the Church must wait upon the Spirit to reveal where true continuity with the gospel lies.

None of this in any way dethrones Christ or Scripture from their unique place at the head of all Christian tradition. The supreme priority of Scripture for all Christian teaching consists, not in its being the *last* word about Jesus and the gospel, but precisely in its being the *first* word. Whatever follows must be in continuity and agreement with that first biblical word, because it is our only access to what God has done for us in Christ. Whether or not the Spirit is speaking in the teaching of the Church must be judged by whether or not that teaching is in continuity and agreement with the scriptural gospel, whether it allows that gospel to be heard and believed in contexts and crises that Scripture does not address and in relation to issues of which the scriptural writers were unaware.

The Holy Spirit who inspired the scriptural writers in one way and inspires the contemporary Church in another will never contradict himself. We shall know when he is speaking now by measuring it by what he said then. However, the continuity between the two will not be restricted to repetitious conformity to the letter of Scripture, but will more often include fresh revelation of and creative insight into the truth in Christ that will bring home in a new way his saving relevance to the life of the Christ of today and the world in which it is set.

The Holy Spirit is himself the living water that flows from the side of Christ, and first reaches and enlivens the apostolic writers who give the Christian tradition its primary and normative expression. The Spirit flows far beyond the Bible, as a great river flows far beyond its headwaters, widening and deepening as it goes, absorbing into itself all sorts of tributaries. It is the work of the Spirit in the Church to see that the living water that comes from Christ purifies what flows into it, rather than being contaminated by it, so that what is flowing broadly in the plains is continuous with what started in the biblical high lands, however much it may have altered in width and depth on the way.

To be more specific, the doctrine of infant baptism and the doctrine of the immaculate conception of the Virgin Mary have it in common that neither is taught explicitly in Scripture. Both emerge at a later stage in the development of the Christian tradition. For a certain kind of Protestant that fact disqualifies both immediately and without further argument. In accordance with what I have just been saying, I would hold that to affirm the appropriateness of infant baptism is scriptural, whereas to affirm the immaculate conception of Mary is not.

To argue the case here in detail would hold us up too long. It must suffice to say that in my view infant baptism is scriptural because its practice corresponds to what Scripture says about the priority of God's grace over the human response to it in the establishment and maintenance of the new covenant in Christ. Thus a good case can be made for accepting infant baptism as a creative explication in the life of the Church of how Christians come to belong to Christ.

On the other hand, I would hold that the immaculate conception of Mary not only has no basis in Scripture, however implicit, but actually obscures what Scripture says about the completeness of Christ's identification with sinners, (cf Rom 8:3, Heb 4:15, II Cor 5:21) by making him the supernaturally sinless Son of a supernaturally sinless mother.

I am of course well aware that Baptists would challenge vigorously my acceptance of infant baptism as in accordance with Scripture and Roman Catholics would as vigorously contest my rejection of the immaculate conception of Mary as non-scriptural in the sense defined. The case for the former and against the latter would need to be argued at length and on its merits.

The point here is simply to maintain that the fact that a doctrine not found in Scripture is taught and believed in the Church in itself neither denies nor affirms its truth. It simply raises the question whether it has that creative continuity with the scriptural witness which is characteristic of the action of the Holy Spirit in relation to Christ. The discerning of that creative continuity, like the discerning of the presence of the Spirit himself, is a far more delicate and subtle business than simply looking for biblical texts to support a position.

The Spirit may well say in the Church what the Bible has not yet said. However, since the Spirit leads us into the same truth in Christ to which the Bible is the primary witness, the Church, if it is open both to the Scriptures and to the Spirit, will be able to discern when there is creative continuity between the two, as she has in fact done at the great doctrinal crisis points in her history.

A parallel point may be made in connection with liturgical and sacramental worship. It is not necessarily true that a celebration of the Lord's Supper which confines itself most rigorously to a detailed repetition of Christ's words and actions in the upper room on Maundy Thursday, in so far as these can be established, reflects most faithfully Christ's intention and purpose in instituting the sacrament. For one thing, to do that involves leaving out the Easter dimension of the Eucharist as it comes to expression within the New Testament itself, as for example in the Emmaus story in Luke 24.

To confine ourselves to a repetition of the Maundy Thursday acts and words of Jesus is to exclude what the Church has learnt from Christ in the Eucharist down the centuries, as that comes to expression in our developed eucharistic liturgies. These liturgies cannot be written off, as they sometimes are by biblicist Protestants, as obscuring complications of an original gospel simplicity. No doubt the distortions of a sinful Church have often been expressed in its liturgical worship. Yet the Church is not only the home of our residual sinfulness; it is also the abiding place of the Holy Spirit who has been the guiding hand in shaping our worship and its liturgical expression. Liturgy can help to make explicit what was still implicit in the words and actions of Jesus on the night before he died. Of course, Jesus' words are for ever central to, and indeed constitutive of the Eucharist, but liturgy at its best is the faithful exegesis by the Spirit in the midst of the prayer of the Church of what Jesus did and said then. It takes what he gave us and declares it to us in all the height and depth of its mystery and glory.

The late Arthur Wallis, the restorationist church leader, for whom I have as much affection in Christ as I have disagreement about the nature of the Church, once said to me that where you have set liturgies and bishops you cannot have the Holy Spirit. Leaving the bishops to take care of themselves for the moment, let me say that those of us who have come to prize liturgical worship more and more, especially if it has a place for freedom and spontaneity within its ordered framework, would argue that liturgy is one of

the chief means by which the Spirit leads us into creative
and continuing contact with the crucified and risen Lord.

So, along with a continuing central emphasis on the fact
that the whole work of the Spirit is related to Christ, we need
to recognise the exercise of his creativity in the tradition of
the Church. We have seen how a one-sided emphasis on the
Son as alone the authoritative expression of God's truth and
salvation can lead to a depreciation of the creativity of the
Spirit, so that we are shut up into a wrong-headed biblicism
that reduces the Spirit to being the guarantor of the written
word, and that treats with suspicion the post-biblical activity
of the Spirit in the Church.

'Who do you say that I am?' It is not Christ himself who
answers that question, nor is it the Church by herself, but the
Spirit in the believing community. He answers it there not
only in the definitive words of Peter or in the teaching of the
apostles. In creative continuity with that teaching he goes on
answering it in the Church of every age. The New Testament
is the Spirit's first word about God's final Word, Christ
himself. As such the word of Scripture has its own unique
and normative place, but the Scriptures are not themselves
God's last word about Christ. The Spirit has had more to tell
us than we could bear to hear at the beginning; in continuity
with Scripture and its explication, he has gone on revealing
Christ in new ways to his people. This creativity of the Spirit
leads us to recognise him as another centre of divine activity,
distinct from both Father and Son, but continually in new
ways bringing home the revelation of Father and Son to
God's people.[8]

The Distinct Personhood of the Holy Spirit
and his Glorification of Father and Son

The Holy Spirit as distinct person is concerned with the
glorification of the Father and the Son. Our second point
about the creativity of the Spirit is to be understood in this
context. 'He will glorify me.' Our response to Jesus is not
Jesus' response to himself, nor does it have its ultimate source

in us. It is the Spirit who glorifies the Son and through him the Father in the Church, giving him a glory, again in Pannenberg's pregnant phrase 'from outside himself.' The Spirit takes from what is in Christ and manifests it in the first place among believers in a way that gives Christ a new glory that he did not have before.

It is basic to Johannine trinitarianism, as we have seen, that the three divine persons do not glorify themselves, but each other, the Son the Father, the Father the Son and the Spirit the Father through the Son. Thus the history of the Church on its positive side – and, of course, it also has a negative side that is shame and not at all glory – is the glory that the Spirit brings to the Son.

He glorifies the Son in the confession of his name, in the proclamation of the word of the gospel, in the celebration of the sacraments and in the whole worship of the Church. The Spirit glorifies the Son in the writings of theologians, in the sanctity of saints, in the fight for social liberation of reformers, and in the death of martyrs. The Spirit glorifies the Son in the conversion and obedience of all the members of the body to the Head, and in the exercise of the gifts and ministries that the Spirit allocates to them. The spiritual theology of the Fathers, the poverty of the first Franciscans, the Christ-centredness of the sixteenth century Reformers, the missionary evangelicalism of Whitefield and the Wesleys, the great missionary pioneers of the nineteenth century, these and countless others – none of them without ambiguity, but all of them with reality – can be described as the glorification of Jesus with a glory that the man of Nazareth never knew. As well as the heavenly glory given him by the Father at his ascension, he has an earthly glory wrought by the Spirit in created people and things, so that they become the firstfruits of the self-offering of the creation to its Creator, Saviour and Lord.

The glory that Christ receives is a little like the glory a subject receives from having his portrait painted by the master artist himself. It is totally inspired by that subject, but nevertheless it gives to that subject a distinction that he did not have before it was painted. The Church by itself could never paint such a portrait of the incarnate Son of God. The artist who is adequate to his subject must be of the same stature as his subject. Only the divine Spirit can adequately glorify the incarnate divine Son in his Church. The glorification of Christ is a trinitarian enterprise in which, according to the will and purpose of the Father who sent him, the Spirit by the conversion and sanctification of the old creation into the new, images the Son and so glorifies him.

It is a still unfinished work: what we have so far are the cartoons in which the master artist foreshadows and prepares his final consummate masterpiece. In a more biblical metaphor, what we have so far are only the firstfruits of the Spirit: there is much more still to come. His work to this point is limited both in quantity and in quality. Still only a minority respond to the Son in the Spirit, and even this response is never total or pure. There remains in all worship, preaching, exercise of gifts and ministries, Christian relationships and enterprises, that which shames Christ rather than glorifies him and which has to be recognised as the work of the flesh rather than the work of the Spirit. Yet with all these necessary qualifications fully taken into account, it remains true that Christ is genuinely glorified by the Spirit in the Church. His firstfruits are a credible promise of the harvest of the whole creation, already reconciled by Christ to the Father, that the Spirit will ultimately gather.

That creation, as it is made responsive to Christ, is the Spirit's gift to the Son. He is fashioning among us the doxology of the created universe; he is teaching us in a thousand ways to sing the new song to the Lamb and to confess in a thousand tongues that Jesus is Lord to the glory of God the Father. This is a real donation of glory from one divine person to another. Here Christ is not just the source but also the recipient of what the Spirit brings to him.

For this to be so requires the personal distinctness of the Spirit from the Son. In that distinctness we can discover the basis of our own freedom to respond to Christ, of the creativity of the Spirit in relation to Christ and of the glory that it is our joy in the Spirit to bring to Christ. No wonder that the whole logic of the New Testament understanding of

God's work among his people pressed it towards an implicitly trinitarian rather than binitarian affirmation of real personal relationships of giving and receiving between the Spirit and the Son. This chapter has tried to give theological reasons for following the biblical lead.

The position I have taken here represents, as I have already indicated, a considerable shift from what I said over ten years ago in *Reflected Glory*. There I emphasised almost exclusively the Spirit's dependence upon the Son, the fact that the whole content of his ministry is to convey Christ and his benefits to us. There is no going back on that here. At a time when charismatic excess and one-sidedness are as prevalent as ever, to relate everything that we say about the Spirit to Christ as the New Testament portrays him is as necessary as ever.

But, taken by itself, this can be understood to imply a one-way subordination of the Spirit to the Son. Christ is the source and the Spirit applies to us what he receives from him. I now see the need to correct that by speaking of a two way co-ordination of Son and Spirit. The Spirit does not only *receive from* Christ, he also *gives to* Christ the glory of a responsive creation he would not otherwise have. The Spirit receives the content of what he conveys to us from outside himself in Christ: Christ receives the earthly crown of glory from outside himself, that is, from the Spirit, just as he receives his heavenly crown of glory from outside himself, from the Father.

His relationship to Christ is not a law that limits the Spirit to repeat and reproduce what he finds in the incarnate Son; rather it is the impulsion that liberates him to an endless spontaneity and creativity that spills over beyond its first biblical expressions and has even more surprises still to come. It is this giving and receiving between Son and Spirit that achieves the Father's purpose in his creation. We have been attempting in the last chapter to give this co-ordination between Son and Spirit a biblical basis, and in this to give it a theological foundation. We shall examine and explain it further as we proceed.

Notes on Chapter Three

(1)　W. Pannenberg, *op. cit.* pp 178–9.

(2)　L.S. Thornton, *The Incarnate Lord*, London, Dacre Press, 1928.

(3)　*ibid.* p 324.

(4)　A.W. Wainwright, *The Trinity in the New Testament*, London, SPCK, 1962, p 218–9.

(5)　Martin Buber, *I and Thou*, ET, Edinburgh, T. & T. Clark, 1937.

(6)　Vladimir Lossky, *The Mystical Theology of the Eastern Church*, ET, London, James Clarke, 1957, pp 169–70.

(7)　Raymond E. Brown, *The Gospel According to St John*, (the Anchor Bible), London, Geoffrey Chapman, 1966, Vol 2, p 716.

(8)　For various approaches to the modern debate about the development of Christian doctrine in relationship to its biblical norms see W.O. Chadwick, *From Bossuet to Newman; the Idea of Doctrinal Development*, Cambridge, C.U.P., 1957 and works there cited. Gabriel Moran, *Theology of Revelation*, London, Burns Oates, 1967. K. Rahner, *Theological Investigations IV*, ET, London, Darton, Longman and Todd, 1966, pp 3ff; and Peter Toon *The Ascension of our Lord*, Nashville, Thomas Nelson, 1984, Chapter Four, pp 73ff.

Chapter Four

The Father's Gift to the Son

What we have said so far is true but incomplete. We have spoken only of how the Holy Spirit functions in relating us to God in Christ. However, before he works in us, the Spirit works in Christ himself. The Holy Spirit comes from the Father to Jesus in his baptism, before he comes to us at Pentecost; it is because he first comes to him that he can then come to us. The Spirit relates the Father to the Son and the Son to the Father before he relates either of them to us. He does it in a way that is revealed to us in what happens in the life of the incarnate Son on earth; further, according to classical trinitarian teaching, the Spirit perpetually relates the Father and the Son to each other within the life of God from eternity to eternity.

We shall leave to a later chapter the difficult question about what we can know and say about the work and being of the Spirit within the eternal life of God himself. In this chapter we shall concentrate on the more immediately accessible question about what we can discover from the gospel story about the way the Spirit functions in the relationship of the heavenly Father to his incarnate Son.

The Baptism of Jesus

With such a question to answer, we must go first to the story of the baptism of Jesus by John in the river Jordan, recounted with remarkable unanimity in all its main features

by all four gospel writers. It is interesting to note in passing
that in the churches of the Christian West the baptism of
Jesus has never been given that pre-eminence among the
mighty acts of God in Christ that it has in the New Testament
itself. In the West the birth of Christ, about which Mark and
John are completely silent, has completely overshadowed his
baptism in liturgical and popular attention. Modern
Anglican liturgy is typical in its relegation of the gospel-
readings of the baptism to the first Sunday after Epiphany.
Epiphany itself, as well as being a cinderella to Christmas, is
devoted to Matthew's story of the coming of the Magi,
which, on any showing, is quite peripheral in importance in
comparison with his baptism, in which his work is
inaugurated and his person revealed. As the eastern
Churches have always well understood, his baptism is his
true epiphany, his showing forth as the Son of God who
comes, endowed with the Spirit, to identify with sinners in
order to set them free.

It is in the context of his baptism that Jesus is designated,
on the one hand, as the Son who receives the Spirit from the
Father, and, on the other, as the one who confers the Holy
Spirit upon us. The witness of John the Baptist is attested in
all four gospels, 'He will baptise you with the Holy Spirit'
(Matt 3:11, Mark 1:8, Luke 3:16, John 1:33). Here to be
baptised in the Spirit does not mean, as in modern
Pentecostalism, a dramatic experience of spiritual renewal
that is attested by the exercise of spiritual gifts. It is to be
understood much more widely as a comprehensive and
corporate inauguration into the new age in which the Spirit
works and rules in a new way, and of which, of course,
renewal experiences and spiritual gifts are a significant part.[1]

In John's account, the baptism of Jesus in water is assumed
in silence. All the emphasis is on the observable descent of the
Spirit upon him. That is what marks him off in the eyes of the
Baptist as the one for whom he has been waiting and
watching, and leads him to testify that Jesus is both the
proto-typical recipient of the Spirit and the bestower of the
new gift of the Spirit that belongs to the new and final age
that is about to begin. 'And John gave this testimony, "I saw

the Spirit come down from heaven as a dove and remain on him. I would not have known him except that the one who sent me to baptise with water told me, 'The one on whom you see the Spirit come down and remain is he who will baptise with the Holy Spirit.' I have seen and I testify that this is the Son of God"' (John 1:32–34).

Jesus both receives and gives the Spirit, so that we see here the sort of reciprocal relationship of interdependence between Son and Spirit that we were outlining at the end of the last chapter. In the present chapter we shall be concentrating on what it means that Jesus *receives* the Spirit and in the next on what it means that he *gives* the Spirit.

According to the passage in John just quoted, the Baptist saw the Spirit 'come down and remain' on Jesus. This implies on the one hand that he entered into a new relationship with the Spirit he had not had before – the Spirit came down – and on the other that it was a permanent relationship – the Spirit remained on him. This was not a temporary anointing but a permanent abiding: the permanent home of the Spirit of God is in the Son of God made flesh.

Although that relationship between Son and Spirit does not of course begin on the day of his baptism, it moves into a decisively new phase then. The Spirit, who has always come from the Father to the Son, comes to him afresh as he sets about his saving work. We shall expound a little later the difference between the pre- and post-baptismal presence of the Spirit in Jesus. At the moment it is enough to note that the most theologically sophisticated of the New Testament accounts, that of John, assumes such a distinction.

Francis Sullivan draws attention to the teaching of Thomas Aquinas, the master medieval schoolman, as being relevant and helpful at this point. Thomas, he says, points out that when Scripture speaks of the coming of a divine person, it never means a movement from absence into presence, since divine persons are by definition always in some sense present. Rather, to say that Father, Son or Spirit comes means that he moves from one kind of presence to another. 'The first point that he [Thomas] makes is that when we talk about the sending of a divine person, we cannot think

of this as a real movement from one place to another, or as a
becoming present where the person was not at all present
before. So it must be a question of the divine person
becoming present where he already is by a new kind of
presence.'[2]

The last phrase is instructive in relation to what happened
between Son and Spirit at the baptism in the Jordan. The
Spirit who has been in Jesus from his birth 'becomes present
where he is already by a new kind of presence.' If that is so, we
have to try to distinguish between the different ways in which
the Spirit is present in the Son.

In *Reflected Glory* I also designated Jesus as both recipient
and donor of the Spirit, but my emphasis at that time was
that he received the Spirit into his human nature as a man,
conferred him upon others in virtue of his divine nature as
Son of God. In the light of further reading and reflection, I
now want to retract that, and say instead that Christ both
received and conferred the Spirit in the oneness of his person
as the Son of God made man. The one who receives the Spirit
at his baptism is not just the man Jesus of Nazareth, but the
one whom John acknowledges at that very point to be the
Son of God. The Spirit is the Gift of the Father to his own
Son, and when that Son is made man, the Spirit is
communicated by him first to his own humanity and then to
ours.

The Spirit that the Father gives his divine Son reaches the
humanity that Son has taken. He is then able to confer the
Spirit on others because his own Spirit-filled humanity is, as
it were, the bridge by which the Spirit can come from him to
us. However, in the baptism of Jesus the basic trinitarian
structure within which the Spirit works and lives comes to
light. He is the personal divine Gift of the divine Father to the
divine Son.

It is interesting in the light of contemporary christological
debate to note that in John a christology in which Jesus is
affirmed unambiguously as the eternal Word or Son of God
made man (John 1:14) co-exists quite harmoniously with a
Spirit-christology in which Jesus is seen as the one who *par
excellence* receives and confers the Spirit. In the modern

discussion an incarnational christology and a Spirit-christoloy have often been treated as mutually exclusive alternatives. The formula of the Council of Chalcedon, the definitive statement of classical christological orthodoxy, makes no reference to the Spirit at all in relation to Christ apart from his involvement in his conception. On the other hand a modern Spirit-christology, like that of G.W. Lampe[3], is explicitly offered as a more viable alternative to the traditional understanding of Jesus as God made man.

In John, however, where the divine identity of Jesus as the only-begotten Son is the basis of his whole message, the descent of the Spirit upon him is as clearly affirmed. The two christologies are seen as complementary rather than contradictory, so that there need be no sense of strain in holding the two together.

Professor James Dunn, who once on his own confession flirted with Spirit-christology as an alternative to incarnational christology, has now happily withdrawn from that position. In one of his more recent writings he criticises a christology concerned to understand Jesus exclusively as a man filled with the Spirit. 'It suffers from the fault of trying to explain the mystery of Christ solely in terms of the Spirit. The Spirit cannot simply be identified with the divinity or deity of Jesus.'[4]

On the positive side Dunn like ourselves wants to affirm the co-existence of the two christologies. He warns us against 'blurring the distinction between a Spirit Christology and a Logos Christology, between a Christology of inspiration and a Christology of incarnation: these are distinct Christologies and both should have a place in any dogmatic synthesis which claims canonical authority'. In the New Testament, he explains, 'A Christology of inspiration was supplemented by, but also retained alongside a Christology of incarnation'.[5] He might have added that in John's gospel we can in fact see the beginning of that integration.

Yves Congar, the Catholic theologian, also insists that we must not allow orthodox incarnational christology to obscure the importance of the different 'comings' of the Spirit to Jesus at his conception, his baptism and his

resurrection. We must, he says, give full weight to the fact
that Jesus is proclaimed not just as the Word made flesh but
as the *Christos*, the one who is anointed by the Spirit, and we
have to understand his person and work in the light of both
these titles.[6] How Congar proposes to relate the two we shall
discover as we proceed.

As we have already noted, the christological formula of
Chalcedon does not speak at all of the Holy Spirit as being
necessarily involved in the constitution of the person of the
God-man, apart from affirming his part in Jesus' conception.
Yet the very fact that he was conceived by the Holy Spirit
itself suggests that the Holy Spirit was very intimately
involved in the joining of the divine and human natures into
one person. It is through the action of the Spirit upon the
common stuff of our humanity which the Son took to himself
that it becomes *capax Dei*, capable of being joined in one
person to the Son of God, who is himself in his eternal
relation to the Father both recipient and donor of the Spirit.

Where that vital reference to the Holy Spirit is omitted,
orthodox christology tends to become very static and
immobile, so that, for example, it finds it very hard to make
room for the dynamic growth and development that were
clearly present in the life of Jesus as depicted in the gospels.
Thomas Aquinas and John Calvin, representing two
mainstreams of Catholic and Reformed theology, both assert
the possession by the incarnate Son of the Holy Spirit in such
fullness and completeness from the moment of his conception that there is no real possibility of his receiving
anything more or new at his baptism. For Thomas and
Calvin, therefore, the voice of the Father and the descent of
the Spirit have to be treated simply as a symbolic
proclamation and manifestation of that which has been
present in all its perfection and fullness from the very first.
Since it all happened at the incarnation, there was nothing
left to happen at the baptism, which is once again, this time
theologically, swallowed up by Christmas.

Congar rightly protests that to treat the baptism in this
way is to obscure the fact that the gospels depict it as a real
kairos in the life of Jesus, one of these moments of

eschatological significance that mark the beginning of a new stage in his life and ministry. In fact, Congar affirms that 'there were successive events in which the Spirit descended upon Jesus as Christ the Saviour. This is clear from the New Testament texts as we read them and interpret their teaching.'[7] One of the chief of these moments, again according to Congar, was his baptism.

He goes on to point out how Luke underlines the new and eventful character of what was happening as Jesus came out of the Jordan by adding, according to many of the best manuscripts, the quotation from Psalm 2:7, 'Today I have begotten you', to the words spoken by the Father in acknowledging Jesus as his Son. That this caused difficulties from the earliest times, because it can be read as casting doubt on Jesus' eternal sonship, is evident from the fact that it is excluded from many other manuscripts and relegated to the margin in many modern translations, especially those of an evangelical character.[8]

Against this Congar rightly points out that, if Luke in fact included the quotation, he could not possibly have meant to indicate by it that Jesus was adopted into sonship for the first time at his baptism – the heresy of adoptionism – since he has already said that Jesus is Son of God by virtue of his virginal conception by the Spirit (1:35). Furthermore, the boy of twelve in the temple shows that he already knows himself to be the Father's Son (2:49). Luke sees the baptism not just as a proclamation of an already fully fledged sonship, but as a decisive new beginning in his relation to the Father, in his awareness of his calling and mission as Son and in his reception of the resources in which that mission was to be accomplished.

From all eternity within the triune life of God, he is the only begotten Son of the Father and neither his conception nor his baptism makes any difference to that. However in his conception by the Spirit he takes humanity to himself and becomes a man who, because he is also the eternal Son, stands in a unique filial relationship to God that is his alone. That relationship is present from his conception and is not changed or affected by his baptism.

In his baptism he who has always been Son and to whom the Spirit has always been given enters into a new phase of his relationship to both Father and Spirit. He is now the Son who for our sake is anointed by the Spirit, so that he may become the firstborn of many brethren, the first man who belongs to the new age that arrives with him, who gives himself in his Father's service to seek, save, shape and remake all the other children whom he will bring to his Father and on whom he will pour out the Spirit. In his baptism the eternal Son made man is anointed as the Messiah of Israel, inaugurated (in the words of Psalm 2, 'begotten') as the promised Son of David who will fulfil all God's promises to his people and pour out the Spirit upon all flesh.

In his baptism the eternal Son who has become the incarnate Son becomes the messianic Son, the Christ. This brings him into a new stage of his relationship to the Father and the Spirit, that fulfils all that has gone before. As Congar himself puts it: 'The event in the Jordan marks the beginning of the messianic era . . . This event brought about no change in Jesus, but it denoted a new *kairos* in the history of salvation. Jesus himself entered a new era, that of which Peter speaks in Acts 10:38. It was disclosed to Jesus by the voice "from heaven." At the same time he also entered in a new way into his consciousness of being the Son, the Messiah and the Servant (see Luke 4:18). This is also borne out by his temptation in the desert and his first proclamation at Nazareth, to which he was led by the Spirit who had come down on him (Luke 4:1).'[9]

If this is so, his baptism was not simply a dramatic manifestation of what had been his from the start; it involved his being given by the Father, in a real dynamic transaction, that which was appropriate to the stage in his life and mission that he had now reached and that would not have been appropriate before. The life of the Son in his interaction with the Father and the Spirit is not lived in the still immobility of static perfection but in the dynamic of constant interchange and mutual giving. He is given in the Spirit exactly what is required at every step of his incarnate career. Not that he had more of the Spirit, in a quantitative sense at one time than at another. He had all of the Spirit from the start, but the Spirit in him responded creatively to the ever changing and developing demands that his life and his death made upon him at every point.

The fullness of the Spirit, both for him and for us, is not immediate possession of a static completeness, but a continuing dynamic self-giving by the Spirit to the person he is filling, which is relevant to where that person is and what he has to do and be. What Paul in Ephesians 5:18 urges upon us, was first of all true of Jesus: he went on being filled with the Spirit. It is that sense of dynamic ongoing relationship between Father, Spirit and incarnate Son that a Spirit-christology is well adapted to express.

The other side of this is, of course, that a Spirit-christology is quite inadequate in itself, apart from an incarnational christology. It is in the eternal Son made flesh and no other that the Spirit takes up his abode in one way at his conception and in another way at his baptism. That is a case that I argued at length against modern Spirit-christologies in *The Forgotten Father*[10], so that it will be enough simply to reaffirm it here.

The particular thrust of our present concern allows us to assume that Christ is to be understood as God's eternal Son made man and to argue that a proper understanding of the Father-Son relationship portrayed in the gospels requires us to take into account, as a factor essential to that relationship, a dynamic donation of the Spirit by the Father to the Son.

The Son is Son, not solely because he shares the divine nature, but because he is in constant interaction with his Father receiving and giving the Holy Spirit. The interaction is infinitely dynamic and creative, so that it is capable of an endless variety of expressions throughout his human life, all the way from Nazareth where the eternal Son becomes human Son through the action of the Spirit in the womb of Mary, to Jordan where he received his sonship afresh in a new messianic dimension that called forth a new outpouring of the Spirit upon him, to Calvary, where he consummated that messianic calling in complete self-giving to the Father. His relation to his Father is indeed eternal; yet it is also pneumatic, that is, it is lived out in the ever active power and creative freshness of the Spirit. It can, therefore, be expressed in all sorts of different ways at different stages of the development of his human life and his messianic mission.

The incarnate Son's reception of the Spirit is adapted to the continuous growth and development that necessarily belong to his human experience. The growth of the boy into the man and the maturing of the man in the midst of his life's work are not negated or threatened by the eternal completeness of the Son of God. The relationship of Father, Son and Spirit does not consist merely of the static sharing of one divine being. It is so dynamic and creative that it can adapt itself to accommodate the real human growing and maturing of the incarnate Son. The self-giving love that binds Father and Son together in the Spirit from eternity to eternity is capable of being expressed through the choice of a twelve-year-old of his central priority, through the descending of the Spirit upon the newly called Messiah, through the days of healing and teaching and the nights of lonely prayer in the villages and hills round Galilee, through the agony of Gethsemane and the final giving of all on the cross.

Calvin and much classical western christology before and after him held that as *man* Jesus grew in the power of the Spirit, but that as *Son of God,* he was eternally complete and so incapable of growth.[11] This raises insoluble problems about how the same person can both grow and mature as a man and be, at the same time, eternally perfect as Son of God. However, such problems need not arise if we understand the Father-Son relationship in the light of what happens at Jesus' baptism. The Father and Son do not so much share a static divine perfection but are related to each other in a constant dynamic giving and receiving of the Spirit. We can then see how the Father can give himself, his love and his power, to the incarnate Son in the Spirit, in a way that is consistent with the Son's real human growth and development.

A human father gives himself to his son in very different ways at different stages of that son's growth from infancy to adult manhood, but at every one of them he recognises him as the son who is being of his being, bone of his bone, flesh of his flesh. The baptism of Jesus invites us to think of the divine Father's giving of himself to the incarnate Son in the Spirit in the same sort of way. The Sonship is eternal and unchanging, but the way Father and Son give themselves to each other in the Spirit is infinitely varied and capable of being adapted to the purpose they are together pursuing.

Three Phases of Imparting

If, however, for our immediate purposes we concentrate on the incarnate Son's experience of the Spirit, we shall, from the New Testament evidence, be able to distinguish and describe three main phases in the imparting of the Spirit to him. The central phase begins at his baptism but it is preceded by an earlier phase and succeeded by a later. To these three we now turn.

1. *The regenerative coming of the Spirit at Jesus' conception.* This is affirmed by the creed in the phrase 'conceived by the Holy Spirit.' Luke's birth story, which, as I said in chapter one, I believe to have history at its heart, is written to show that it is the Holy Spirit who brings the Son of God to birth in our humanity.

In Luke 1:35 it is explicitly affirmed that the child to be born of Mary can be called the Son of God, because he owes his generation to the action of the Holy Spirit upon his mother, and not to any human father. In this context 'Son of God' means one whose human life has been brought into being by the direct action of God through the Holy Spirit. In this context Luke makes no mention of any pre-incarnate external existence of God's Son. However, unlike Pannenberg[12], I do not see that there is any inconsistency between Luke's nativity story and John's full blown incarnational christology. It is, of course, true that Luke does not relate his nativity story to incarnational christology any more than John relates his incarnational christology to the story of the virginal conception of Jesus. But the fact that the two approaches are not explicitly related to each other by the gospel writers does not mean that they are inherently inconsistent.

For our purposes here, we should note the congruence between what Luke says about the birth of Christ and what John says about the rebirth of Christians. It is well known that there is a variant reading of the text of John 1:13, which relates it to Jesus rather than to us, so that it affirms that Jesus himself is 'born, not of natural descent, or of a human decision or of a husband's will, but of God,' which would amount to an explicit Johannine endorsement of Jesus' virginal conception.

However, even if we remain with the accepted reading of the verse, which has the support of an overwhelming majority of the most trustworthy manuscripts, the phrase 'not by the will of a husband (*andros*)' does suggest that there is an indirect allusion to the virgin birth of Jesus. The passage was in fact so understood by early writers like Ignatius, Justin Martyr and Irenaeus.[13]

Hoskyns and Davy in their great commentary on John sum the matter up carefully: 'The evangelist employs phraseology actually used of or obviously suggestive of the virgin birth, transferring or applying it to the desired spiritual miracle of Christian regeneration, but in such a way that the reference to the miraculous birth of Jesus is preserved and presumed.'[14] In other words there is a regenerative activity of the Holy Spirit, which Luke affirms in relation to Christ and that John affirms in relation to Christians. John, however, does it in a way which clearly suggests that our spiritual rebirth by the Spirit is analogous to his physical birth of Mary by the same Spirit.

Note that this aspect of the Spirit's work, first in Jesus and then in us, is properly described as *re*generative or re-creative rather than simply creative. The humanity that is joined to the Son of God by the action of the Spirit is not created out of nothing; it is born of Mary. What God does in sending Jesus is not to reject or abolish all that has gone before in order to begin afresh. The humanity that he takes is the old humanity of Adam, shaped and made ready in the long history of

Israel, and now taken from Mary and given a capacity and an ability that are not native to it. It is the capacity and ability to be so united with God that it becomes the means of his self-expression and self-giving to the world.[15]

If it took nothing less than an action of God in Peter to enable him to confess Jesus at Caesarea Philippi, how much more did it take an act of God the Holy Spirit in the womb of Mary to regenerate and vivify the humanity that came from her, to enable it to be united in one person with the eternal Son of God.

The gift of the Spirit to the Son in his conception, is the gift of this new humanity. On the one hand it is our humanity subject to all its weaknesses, temptations and external and internal tensions. On the other hand it has been regenerated by the Spirit and made capable of receiving from and responding to God, so as to give authentic expression to his life, love and power in genuinely human terms. In that humanity, thus regenerated by the Spirit, the Son receives from and obeys the Father.

What the regenerating Spirit does in us is dependent upon what he has first done in the humanity of Christ. As his human nature is regenerated by the Spirit in Mary's womb, so by the action of the same Spirit, we are born again from above, so that we can discern, respond to and enter the kingdom of God (John 3:3,5). Everyone who becomes a Christian does so only as a result of the regenerative action of the Holy Spirit upon him.

Paul's equivalent to John's 'new birth' language is his speaking, for example in II Corinthians 5:17, of a *kaine ktisis*, a new creation. The word *kaine* means not 'novel', but 'renewed'. It is not the kind of new beginning that has little or no relationship to what went before but rather a supernatural liberation of the old creation, so that it is enabled by God to respond to God.

In a later chapter, we shall look more closely at what this means for us. Our concern at the moment is to see that before the Spirit comes to regenerate us he comes to regenerate the humanity of the incarnate Son of God. To establish this, as we have seen, the nativity narrative of Luke is very

important. Although it does not speak of the Son's eternal
pre-existence, it does make it quite clear that he is not an
ordinary man who at some point of his career achieves or
acquires divine sonship – the teaching known as adoptionism.
From the start he has his origin in the mystery of God who
intervenes in the processes of human conception to make a
radical new beginning by his Spirit.

In Christ as prototype and promise for all of us, our sinful
humanity is regenerated into a new relationship to God by
the Holy Spirit. Or, to put the same thing in Pauline terms,
'The first Adam was of the dust of the earth, the second
Adam was from heaven' (I Cor. 15:47).

2. *The Spirit comes to Jesus at his baptism to anoint him
as Messiah.* The regenerating Spirit is also the messianic
Spirit. Messiah or Christ means 'the anointed one'; that with
which he is anointed is the Holy Spirit; the place and time of
that anointing is his baptism in the Jordan.

There he is anointed with God's presence and power in a
way that will enable him to be the servant of the Lord, who
will act savingly on behalf of his people. He takes his stand
with repentant sinners by sharing the water of their baptism.
He will set them free from sin by going to the cross as the
Lamb of God who takes away the sin of the world (John
1:29). Thus he will enable them to receive and witness in the
same Spirit that anointed him, so that they will become
Christ-ians, the messianic, anointed people.

Jesus' reflection on all that has happened to him in the
Jordan and the wilderness comes to expression in his sermon
in the synagogue at Nazareth, where he appropriates to
himself and his ministry the words of Isaiah 61:1-2: 'The
Spirit of the Lord is on me, because he has anointed me to
preach good news to the poor. He has sent me to proclaim
freedom for the prisoners and recovery of sight for the blind,
to release the oppressed, to proclaim the year of the Lord's
favour' (Luke 4:18-19).

He has been anointed Messiah to be God's servant in
liberating his people and it is in the power of the Spirit who
has come upon him that he fulfils his task. Thus, if the words
of the Father at the baptism, 'Today I have begotten you'

(Luke 3:22, RSV margin), are indeed part of the original text, they refer neither to the divine Son who is eternally begotten of the Father, nor to the regenerate new man, who came to birth thirty years before, but rather to the messianic Son. It is from the day of his baptism that he begins his liberating work.

Jesus the Messiah is the one who is anointed with the Spirit to liberate others. He was always reluctant to accept the title in case it should be misunderstood in terms of dominating power and privilege, rather than in the context of liberating servanthood. The central question being decided in his temptation in the wilderness is what kind of Messiah he will choose to be. In the sequel the outcome is crystal clear. He is not Messiah to turn stones into bread to feed his own hunger. He is not Messiah to enter into compromising covenants with the forces of evil in order to gain universal power. He is not Messiah in order to perform sensational signs and wonders that will establish his special status with God in his own eyes and in the eyes of others.

All these false ways he rejects and leaves behind in the wilderness. At Nazareth he publicly affirms that his way of being Messiah is the way of liberating service to others in obedience to his Father. He remains faithful to that decision all the way to the cross.

The Holy Spirit is the anointing power of that liberation. While this truth does not often come to explicit expression in the synoptic account of his ministry, it is at least hinted at in Matthew 12:28: 'But if I drive out demons by the Spirit of God, then the kingdom of God has come upon you.' Here, the liberating work of Jesus and the kingly rule of God are closely connected. In Acts 10:38 also the anointing of the Spirit is seen as the equipment of Jesus for his liberating work: 'God anointed Jesus of Nazareth with the Holy Spirit and with power, and he went about doing good and healing all who were under the power of the devil, because God was with him.' Again spiritual anointing and liberating ministry are brought into the closest connection.

Here I would appeal to Jesus' own principle which applies to much more than marriage: 'What God has joined together, let not man put asunder' (Matthew 19:6). On the one side are charismatic Christians who constantly seek the anointing of the Holy Spirit, but who have yet to show how willing they are to become involved in God's liberating activity in the world. On the other there are social, activist Christians, who want to liberate the oppressed, without receiving the messianic Spirit, who alone will enable them to do so effectively. Oh for the day when the charismatics become the liberators and the liberators become charismatic, because Jesus was both! It is within this context of Spirit-anointed servanthood that sends you to others to set them free on every level, that the charismatic dimension of the gospel and the right exercise of the gifts of the Spirit can alone be properly understood and healthily experienced.

In Hebrews 9:14 the work of the cross itself is seen as the climax of this anointed messianic servanthood which sets others free, so that they may themselves become God's anointed servants. 'How much more then will the blood of Christ, who through the eternal Spirit offered himself unblemished to God, cleanse our consciences from acts that lead to death, so that we may serve the living God.'

Our relationship to God, our obedience to God, our service of God all derive from him. Because his obedient liberating servanthood was in the power of the anointing messianic Spirit who came upon him in the Jordan, our Christian life and ministry must have their source in his Holy Spirit. For, in that Spirit who brings Christ's liberation to us and sends us to liberate others in the name of Jesus, we also have been baptised (I Cor 12:13).

3. *The Spirit transfigures Jesus at his resurrection.* This is the phase of the Spirit's activity in Jesus that we have not yet mentioned. As well as the regenerating and anointing work of the Spirit we have already described, there is a transfiguring work of the Spirit in the risen but still human Lord.

Before Jesus gives the Spirit to others at Pentecost, he himself receives the Spirit afresh in a way that is distinct from the way he received him at his conception and at his baptism, although of course the regenerating and the anointing

THE FATHER'S GIFT TO THE SON   105

remain. In connection with the completion of his saving work, his resurrection and his ascension to the Father's right hand, there has been a new work of the Spirit in him, which results in the transfiguration and sanctification of his humanity in a new way and to a new degree.

That is part of the New Testament tradition about the relation of Jesus and the Spirit. It comes to expression in Acts 2:33: 'Exalted to the right hand of God, *he has received from the Father the promised Holy Spirit*, and has poured out what you now see and hear.' The clear meaning is that the Spirit who has now been poured out on the disciples was first poured out upon the ascended Jesus.

The same strand of teaching is to be found in Paul. In Romans 1:4 he says that Jesus 'through the Spirit of holiness was declared with power to be the Son of God by his resurrection from the dead.' Käsemann comments: 'The Spirit of holiness is the power in virtue of which Jesus is appointed the Son of God, just as the oral tradition of Jesus' baptism spoke of his messianic appointment by the Holy Spirit.'[16]

Here Son of God means neither the eternal Son of Johannine Christology, nor the Spirit-generated Son of Luke's nativity story, nor yet the anointed Messianic Son of the Jordan baptism, but rather the Son who is exalted to the exercise of God's power in a transfigured and transformed resurrected humanity: this is seen in terms of a fresh giving of the Spirit to him.

So also in I Corinthians 15:45: 'The last Adam became a life-giving Spirit.' The *eschatos Adam*, the ultimate man, is the one who has been transfigured and sanctified by the Spirit so as to fulfil at last God's purpose for the whole of humanity. As such he is so full of the Spirit of divine self-giving that he pours out upon others his transfigured and fulfilled humanity, so that they also may be changed into sanctified and fulfilled people.

He who, as anointed Messiah, obeyed his Father as the humble servant of the Lord, now reigns in glory in his resurrected manhood and in the power of the same Spirit. He has received all authority in heaven and earth from the

Father (Matthew 28:18). The eschatological Spirit of resurrection and glorification has been poured out upon him. As a result, he at Pentecost pours out the same Spirit upon the depressed and defeated disciple company so that the last days are seen to have begun (Acts 2:27), although not yet to have come to their consummation. We have the Spirit as the firstfruits (*aparche* – Rom 8:23) and the first instalment (*arrabon* – Ephes 1:14) of our resurrected and transfigured humanity, as a promise that what is still lacking will surely follow.

Thus we see Jesus regenerated, anointed, and transfigured by the same Holy Spirit. The eternal Son who becomes man in him evidences his sonship in one way in his birth, in another at his baptism and in yet another at his resurrection. He who from before all worlds is the Son of God related to his Father by the mutual giving and receiving of the Spirit, expresses that spiritual relationship in different ways at different stages of his human history, in his generation, his messianic anointing and his glorification.

Putting the same thing the other way round, the Spirit who eternally dwells in the Son by the gift of the Father, expresses his indwelling in the incarnate Son by the regeneration, anointing and glorification of his humanity.

These three phases of the Spirit's work are never entirely separate from one another, because the one Spirit is the agent of them all. The regeneration is with a view to the anointing and the glorification. The anointing is the anointing of an already regenerate humanity, as he enters upon the path of servanthood that will lead him to his glorification. His glorification is itself the destination and the perfecting of the other two and so depends upon them.

To call him Jesus Christ the Lord encapsulates the three phases in the three names. Jesus is the name given in the context of his conception by the Spirit. To call him Christ is to speak of his messianic anointing. *Kurios,* Lord, is the title of the one who is exalted to glory with the Father. All three are the names of the one human and divine person who bears them.

The fact that he is first born of the Spirit, then after a time of obscurity anointed by the Spirit, and finally, after his ministry and death, glorified by the Spirit has to do with the special unfolding of his human story, and does not provide any basis for a temporally separated succession of experiences of the Spirit by us. I did not reject a second blessing view of the work of the Spirit in *Reflected Glory* in order to embrace a threefold succession of experiences here.

The Christ who breathes the Spirit upon us now is simultaneously, completely and eternally the incarnate, regenerated, anointed and glorified Son. The Spirit, whom we receive from him, is the Spirit who has perfected all his work in Christ's humanity and, on that basis, can do his work in us in whatever order and way his love for us directs.

Our messianic empowering as Christians can begin from the moment of our regeneration, or it can become manifest much later. New Christians can begin to shine with something of Christ's resurrection glory as easily as old ones. On the basis of Paul's strictures on the Corinthians one could even ask whether it is possible to be anointed without being regenerate, to exercise charismatic gifts without being born again. For he addresses those whose possession of spiritual gifts he acknowledges as 'not spiritual but of the flesh' (I Cor 3:1). Before reaching such a conclusion, however, we need to notice that, if, on the negative side, he calls them 'men of the flesh,' he also calls them in the next phrase 'babes in Christ,' which is much more positive. From all of which we are certainly entitled to conclude that their charismatic potentialities were much more developed than other basic factors of their new life in Christ, especially their transformation into his likeness.

The Son's Response in the Spirit to the Father

We need to be clear that the Spirit can do his work in whatever order he will, or that we are open to receive. What he does in us is always the same as what he did in Christ: he

regenerates, he anoints, he transforms. What happens to us
in the Spirit is totally dependent on what first happened to
him.

Jesus receives the Spirit from the Father, and in the Spirit
he responds to the Father. The Father is both the source from
which the Spirit comes to him and the one to whom in the
Spirit Jesus gives himself in all his living and dying. We, in
turn, receive the Father's Spirit from Jesus and we respond in
the Spirit to the Father through him. In him, not in us, the
work of the Spirit in humanity has been completed; in us it
has only just begun. What has been started in us is what has
been completed in him. Because he is regenerate, we are
regenerated. Because he is anointed with divine authority, so
are we. Because in the Spirit he is the *eschatos Adam*, the
ultimate man, the Spirit brings that new manhood from him
to us.

Our response to him is not a novel response, not something
we invent or originate. We simply give back to him in the
Spirit what we have first received from him in the Spirit. The
work of the Spirit is to take the regenerated humanity in
which he related to *Abba* in sonship, the messianic humanity
that enables him to serve *Abba* on earth, the glorified
humanity that sits at the right hand of *Abba's* throne, and to
transfer it to us. As a result we begin to become adopted sons
and daughters who respond to the Father and the Son in the
trust and obedience that the Spirit has brought us from Jesus.
We begin to become the messianic children of God who are
empowered by the Spirit for service and suffering, as Jesus
was before us. We begin to become the changed and
transformed children, who are being changed into the family
likeness that Christ already bears from one degree of glory to
another (II Cor 3:18).

Christ has already received from and responded to the
Father on our behalf in our humanity. The work of the Spirit
is simply to bring over to us from Christ what he has done for
us, so that it can be done in us as well. 'What do you have that
you did not receive?', asks Paul of the Corinthians (I Cor 4:7).
What do we give to God that has not first been given to us by
God? The Spirit is the Gift of the Father who comes to us

through the humanity of the incarnate Son. He is the Giving Gift, because it is his work ultimately to give to our humanity all that is in Christ's.

I much appreciate Professor T.F. Torrance's emphasis on the fact that Christ has made an acceptable response to God on behalf of all of us, because we could not make it by ourselves. Jesus is not only God's gracious 'Yes' to us: he has spoken, on behalf of all men, our responding 'Yes' to God. As Torrance himself puts it: 'He [Jesus] has acted in your place in the whole range of your human life and activity, including your personal decisions and your responses to God's love, and even your acts of faith. He has believed for you, fulfilled your human response to God, even made your personal decision for you, so that he acknowledges you before God as one who has already responded to God in him, who has already believed in God through him, and whose personal decision is already implicated in Christ's self-offering to the Father.'[17]

I find Torrance most helpful in explaining how our response to God is dependent upon Christ's response on our behalf. He gives christological depth to the assertion that we cannot respond by ourselves. He expounds in contemporary terms the basic Pauline insight that being saved by grace through faith means that God has to work not just on our behalf outside us but within us as well.

I am bound to say, however, that Professor Torrance leaves me dissatisfied with his failure to take adequate account of the equally important New Testament insight, that Christ's response on my behalf has to become my own response to Christ before it can take effect in me. It is indeed true that I cannot respond by myself till Christ has responded for me; it is also true that I must answer for myself and that I have not done so until the Spirit brings Christ's vicarious 'Yes' to God on my behalf, and makes it available to me on my side of the relationship. It is then that I say my own 'Amen' in the Spirit to the answer he has given, and glorify him as I say it.

To return to our model in Matthew 16, it is of course true that Peter's confession of Christ is inconceivable and incomprehensible apart from Jesus' own response to God. It is the implications of that which Torrance expounds so helpfully. Nevertheless the confession is still made by Peter to Jesus; it is the fact that he confesses Christ, not that Christ makes a confession on his behalf, that makes him the rock on which the Church can be built (v 18).

Christ has in his speaking, his living and his suffering brought humanity's 'Yes' to God on behalf of us all. Only because he has said it for me, can I say it for myself; but I still do need to say that 'Yes' for myself, so that I may benefit from what Christ has done for me. It is the Spirit who comes from Christ to me who lets me say my 'Yes' to his 'Yes'. My 'Yes' is not just an echo of his – one of Torrance's favourite phrases. My 'Yes' is rather the result and consequence of his. In my 'Yes' the Spirit makes Christ's work fruitful in me in a way that it has not been before and thus brings him a glory that he did not have before.

To take another biblical example, the martyrdom of Stephen, as described in Acts 7, is totally shaped by and dependent on the death of Jesus, to the extent that Stephen dies with words on his lips that are almost the same as those of Jesus. Of course the death of Stephen is not the atoning vicarious sacrifice that reconciles humanity to God. That happened once for all at Calvary. However, even if Stephen's martyrdom does not have that surpassing glory that is unique to Calvary, it does have a glory of its own. It is Stephen's Amen to what Christ did for him on Calvary. It shows that what Christ did for him has taken such effect within him that he is ready to give his life to be faithful to it. Christ's own sacrifice has a new glory because in the Spirit it creates this response in Stephen.

What Christ has done *for* me has to be brought from him to me and done *in* me in a way that is authentic both to him and to me, so that my response is true to him and is yet my own. The Spirit is able to bring this about, because he is both the Spirit who has shaped the humanity of Jesus and the Spirit who has creative access to the springs of my being and can reshape them in the likeness of Christ.

The worship, the thinking, the life and witness of the

Church are not the word of God in the way that the incarnate
Son is. But they are the response of the Church to that
incarnate Word. They are the answer we give to what he says
to us and does for us. It is an answer that we give to him for
ourselves in the creativity of the Spirit who comes to us from
him.

So much modern Christian writing and spirituality have so
overemphasised the centrality of the human response to
Christ that we should be grateful to Professor Torrance and
the whole Barthian tradition, for which at this point he
speaks, for insisting that Christ has answered for us when we
have nothing to say for ourselves. Nevertheless, the fragment
of truth buried deep in that modern emphasis is its insistence
that it is not enough that a response to God should be made
for me by Jesus, but what he has done for me, I need to go on
and do for myself.

Even Calvin, the archpriest of divine sovereignty,
emphasised that very point in the first chapter of the third
book of his *Institutes*. 'As long as Christ remains outside of
us and we are separated from him, all that he has suffered and
done for the salvation of the human race remains useless and
of no value for us.'[18] And again: 'Until our minds become
intent upon the Spirit, Christ, so to speak, lies idle because we
coldly contemplate him as outside ourselves – indeed far
from us.'[19] In other words, to use our own terminology, it is
the Spirit who brings what Christ has done to our side of the
relationship. Only when he does that do we benefit from it.

It is perhaps significant that Professor Torrance's failure
to distinguish clearly enough between Christ's response to
God made for us and our response to Christ made for
ourselves, goes alongside a wider failure to distinguish clearly
enough between the work of the Spirit and the work of
Christ. Of course the Spirit is in all his works and ways the
Spirit of Christ. That is why everything that he creates in me
has its origin and prototype in Jesus. If, as we have argued,
the Spirit is a centre of personal action distinct from Christ,
then there is room for him to create and evoke in me a
response that I can bring to Christ for myself and will give
him glory.

My obedience, my faith, my will to respond do indeed derive from what Christ has done for me. The Spirit brings them to me, enables me to affirm and say my 'Yes' to them. He gives them such fresh creative expression in the particular setting of my life that I can bring them to Christ as the authentic offering of my praise, my witness, my self-giving. The balance between what Christ does *for* me and what the Spirit then does *in* me to enable me to respond to him is, I submit, best maintained in the context of the kind of real personal distinction between Son and Spirit that it is a main concern of this book to make.

Where that distinction is not made, it is easy to yield to the tendency to overemphasise Christ's work for us at the expense of the Spirit's work in us that we have discerned in Torrance. Where, on the other hand, as happens in some pentecostal and charismatic teaching, the work of the Spirit is treated in too great isolation from the work of Christ, we shall almost certainly find the opposite tendency – to be too interested in what the Spirit does in our experience at the expense of what Christ has done for us on the cross.

Where then have we got to? It might perhaps help to set it out in the form of a diagram.

FATHER

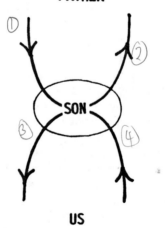

US

Figure One

In Figure One above, the action of the Spirit is indicated by the lines and the arrows. There are two descending and ascending movements which meet in the Son. In the upper half-circle the Spirit first descends from the Father to the incarnate Son as his Gift to him. The Father gives himself to the Son in the Spirit. One of the most significant moments of that giving is at his baptism in the Jordan.

The upper half-circle is complete only when the arc ascends again to the Father from which it started. The Spirit comes down from the Father to the Son, but he also ascends from the Son to the Father when, in obedience and sacrifice, the Spirit-filled Son gives himself to the Father. Thus the Spirit who is first the Father's Gift to the Son is then the Son's responsive Gift to the Father.

Turning now to the lower half-circle, we see that not only does the Father give the Spirit to the incarnate Son, but through that Son the Spirit is also given to us whose humanity the Son shares. On the lower half-circle the descent of the Spirit of the Father from Christ to us is what began to happen on the day of Pentecost and has gone on happening ever since. We receive from him the regeneration, the messianic anointing and the sanctifying transformation that were wrought by the Spirit in his humanity and are now to be worked out in ours.

The Spirit who comes to us from Christ is the Spirit of self-giving and obedience, so that by him we are caught up into offering ourselves to God in the trust, obedience and service that are the results in our lives of Christ's own offering to the Father. That is why the lower half circle also turns upwards in offering to God. The Spirit who through Christ comes from the Father enables us through Christ to offer ourselves to the Father 'as living sacrifices holy and pleasing to God' (Rom 12:1).

The lower half-circle is in the closest dependence upon the upper. We receive the Spirit only because Christ did; we offer ourselves in the Spirit only because Christ offered himself for us. The two half-circles are not, however, to be merged. What the Spirit did in Christ is the final manifestation of the Father's glory. And in what the Spirit does in us Christ is also glorified in a different way. By the Spirit who regenerated his humanity, we are born again; by the Spirit who anointed him in the Jordan with divine authority for a messianic task, we are anointed with power from on high to be his people; by the Spirit who raised him from the dead we are raised up to a new and holy life with him. In what happens to us what happened to him bears fruit. Our 'Yes' to Christ in the Spirit is the demonstration of Christ's 'Yes' to God in the Spirit.

So, to conclude our chapter, the Spirit is, in Augustine's language the bond (*nexus*) and link (*vinculum*) between the Father and the Son (upper half-circle) and between Father, Son and us (lower half-circle). He takes what is the Father's and gives it to the Son in his baptism; he takes what is the Son's and gives it to us in ours. He is the Giving Gift of the Father to the Son and of both to us. Having received such a Gift, what can we do with it except what Jesus himself did – give ourselves to God!

Notes on Chapter Four

(1) See James D.G. Dunn, *Baptism in the Holy Spirit*, London, SCM Press, 1970, especially Chapter Two, pp 23ff.
Compare also Karl Barth, *Church Dogmatics*, IV,4 (Fragment), ET, Edinburgh, T & T Clark, 1969, pp 53ff.

(2) Francis A. Sullivan SJ, '*Charisms and Charismatic Renewal*, Dublin, Gill and Macmillan, 1982, p 70.

(3) Most extensively in his notable Bampton Lectures, *God as Spirit*, the central thesis of which we discussed above in Chapter Two.

(4) J. G. D. Dunn, 'Rediscovering the Spirit – 2' in *Expository Times* for October 1982, p 14.

(5) *ibid.* p 15–16.

(6) Yves Congar, *I Believe in the Holy Spirit*, ET, London, Geoffrey Chapman, 1983, Vol 3 pp 165–71.

(7) *ibid.* p 166.

(8) The New International Version, which we are using throughout this book does not even acknowledge it in the margin as a possible variant reading.

(9) *ibid.* p 167–8.

(10) *op. cit.* pp 97ff.

(11) John Calvin, *Institutes of the Christian Religion*, Vol 2, ET,

(John T. McNeill, ed) (Philadelphia, Westminster Press, 1960, Book Two, Chapter XIV, pp 483–4.

(12) W. Pannenberg, op cit. p 143.

(13) E. Hoskyns and F. N. Davey (ed.), The Fourth Gospel, London, Faber & Faber, 1947, p 163.

(14) ibid. p 165.

(15) I here follow Karl Barth who, in line with some of the Greek Fathers, and much modern theology held that the human nature that Christ assumed was fallen humanity regenerated by the Spirit, cf. Karl Barth, Church Dogmatics, I, 2, ET, Edinburgh, T. & T. Clark, 1956, pp 53ff.

(16) Ernst Käsemann, Commentary on Romans, ET, London, SCM Press, 1980, pp 12–13.

(17) Thomas F. Torrance, The Mediation of Christ, Exeter, Paternoster Press, 1983, p 104.

(18) John Calvin, Institutes of the Christian Religion, Vol I, ET ed. J. T. McNeill, Philadelphia, Westminster Press, 1960, Vol 1, p 537.

(19) ibid. p 541.

Chapter Five

Who Gives the Gift?

In the light of all that we have been saying, such a question seems hardly to need a chapter to itself. Can it not be answered in a single sentence? The Father gives the Spirit to the Son first and then to all of us who believe in the Son. This is what is clearly implied in what happened in the baptism of Jesus and it is a statement with which all trinitarian Christians would readily agree. However, although all agree that the Father is the Giver of the Spirit, the matter becomes more complicated when we raise the question as to whether the Son also is involved in the giving of this Gift. Is the Son just the recipient or is he also, in some sense, the donor of the Spirit?

To raise that question is to enter one of the central areas of long-standing controversy between the Churches of the eastern Orthodox tradition and the Churches of the West, both Roman Catholic and Protestant. These two sets of Churches have for long answered the question about the part of the Son in the giving of the Spirit in two quite different ways – so different indeed that on this issue they have broken their communion with one another for nearly a thousand years.[1]

Both sides agree that God the Father gives the Spirit. For the eastern Orthodox it is indeed one of the defining characteristics of the Father that he is the source and origin of both the Son and the Spirit. A Father and a Son are both of the same being and nature, but they differ from each other because the Father gives being to his Son and the Son has his being from his Father. And, so the East has always argued, as the Father is the sole source of the Son, so the Father is also the sole source of the Spirit. It belongs uniquely to the person of the Father to originate the other two: it belongs to the persons of the Son and the Spirit that in different ways they have their being not from themselves but from the Father. To use the language of the Creeds the Son is 'eternally begotten of the Father' and the Spirit 'proceeds from the Father.' So to the question, 'Who gives the Spirit?', the East has tended to answer, sometimes with great vehemence, 'the Father alone'.

The western approach is different. It begins from the fact that Father and Son share completely the one divine being and nature. Just because the Son has his being and nature from the Father, everything that the Father is, the Son is also, and everything that the Father does both in eternity and in time the Son does also. Thus, by this logic, if the Father is the giver of the Spirit, so also is the Son. So to the question, 'Who gives the Spirit?', the western Churches have for many centuries answered, 'the Father *and* the Son'.

It is the implications of that controversy that we shall be examining in this chapter. At first sight we may be forgiven for thinking that the question is so highly technical and hopelessly academic that we may safely leave it to the theological pundits who have a taste for that sort of thing. However, as we persevere, we shall begin to see that important issues are involved which have their source in the biblical gospel, which have significant practical consequences for Christian worship and life, and which are highly relevant to the reconciliation of eastern and western Christianity, in a way that would expose the riches of these two great traditions to each other. What has not been possible for a thousand years is beginning to be possible today. It is, therefore, worth looking at what first divided them in order to see what might now unite them.

The Biblical Evidence

To make sure that we keep our feet on firm gospel ground, we should look first at what the New Testament itself has to say. There we shall find in the farewell discourses of Jesus in John 14–16 some sensitive reflections on how the Father and the Son are involved in the coming of the Spirit. Even if, as some scholars argue, the language of these chapters comes directly from the apostle rather than from Jesus himself, they certainly express faithfully how Jesus himself saw his part in the coming of the Paraclete-Spirit.

We may summarise the teaching of these chapters by saying that it is the Father who sends the Spirit and his coming is conditioned by, and is in the most intimate connection with, the person of Jesus and with the completion of his work on the cross and in the resurrection.

Thus in John 14:16 Jesus says: 'I will ask the Father and he will give you another Counsellor.' Here the giver is quite clearly the Father, but his giving is in response to the prayer of the Son. In 14:26 Jesus speaks of 'the Counsellor, the Holy Spirit, whom the Father will send in my name.' The phrase 'in my name' means in response to all that Jesus is and stands for. The central verse, that was to play a key role in the long medieval controversy is John 15:26, out of which contending theologians often read far more than it actually contains. 'When the Counsellor comes, whom I will send to you from the Father, the Spirit of truth, who proceeds from the Father, he will testify about me.' Here it is Jesus who sends the Spirit but it is 'from the Father' that he is sent: it is from the Father as his ultimate source and origin that he '*proceeds*.' The phrase about the Spirit in the Nicene creed, 'who *proceeds* from the Father,' is derived from this verse.

In 16:7–8 we are again told that the coming of the Paraclete is dependent upon the completion of the work of the Son. Here, for once, the part of the Father is not explicitly mentioned. 'Unless I go away the Counsellor will not come to you, but if I go I will send him to you.' All these pre-resurrection promises are fulfilled in 20:22 where it is the risen Jesus who on Easter evening breathes in the disciples the promised Holy Spirit in the context of his passing on to them the mission that he himself has received from the Father (v 21).

In the other three gospels the promise of the Spirit comes, as we have seen, in the context of Jesus' baptism by John who says of him: 'He will baptise you with the Holy Spirit', whom, of course, Jesus has himself just received from the Father (Matt 3:11, Mark 1:8, Luke 3:16). The Gift that he passes on to us is the Gift that has come to him from the Father.

At the beginning of Acts the Spirit is described as 'the gift my Father promised' (1:4), while the delivery of that gift is ascribed to the ascended Jesus in Acts 2:33: 'Exalted to the right hand of God, he has received from the Father the promised Holy Spirit and has poured out what you now see and hear.'

So the New Testament witness, expressed particularly by John and confirmed by the other writers who refer to the matter, is that the Spirit is sent *by* and *from* the Father and also *through* and even *by* the incarnate Son, Jesus. The relationship of the part that the Father takes in sending the Spirit to the part that the Son takes is left sufficiently undefined and open for the two sides in the later controversy to arrive at opposing conclusions from the same set of biblical texts.

It was, in fact, passionately held opposing positions on this question that was in the twelfth century to lead to the great schism between the Orthodox East and the Catholic West. And, since the doctrine of the Trinity in general and the relation of Father and Son to the sending of the Spirit in particular were not major, controversial issues in the sixteenth century, the churches of the Reformation, Lutheran, Calvinist and Anglican alike, have traditionally followed the western line on this question. The outward and visible sign of the disagreement is, as we shall soon see, the variant forms of the Nicene creed that are used in worship in the eastern and western Churches.

It is important to realise that we are not dealing only with ancient history. In the last century, and particularly since the Russian revolution of 1917, the Orthodox Churches have been brought into fresh contact with the Churches of the West and have participated in the ecumenical movement. So the debate about the Son and the Spirit that was closed for centuries has been reopened in a positive and promising way. Moreover, the ensuing discussion offers a fresh perspective on questions which are important not only in an ecumenical context, but also for the life and witness of all the Churches at a time of fresh interest in and openness to the person and work of the Holy Spirit. We shall by no means be wasting our time if we try to see where on both sides right and wrong lie.

The Eastern Position –
the Father Alone Breathes out the Spirit

First, then, a little potted history. The first credal statement about the source of the Spirit dates from the Council of Constantinople in 381 where the creed we call Nicene was given its final form. The third article about the Spirit runs as follows: 'We believe in the Holy Spirit, the Lord, the giver of life, who proceeds from the Father, with the Father and Son is worshipped and glorified, who spoke through the prophets.'

We have already noted the inadequacy of this statement as a summary of the New Testament material about the Spirit and his work, but we should now note more positively what it does say. Firstly, it clearly implies the *divinity* of the Holy Spirit, by applying to him the divine title, *Kurios,* Lord, and by claiming for him the same worship that is due to the Father and the Son.

Secondly, it says that he 'proceeds from the Father.' The Spirit has his source in the Father just as the Son has. The Son is 'eternally begotten from the Father' and the Spirit 'proceeds from the Father' – a quotation from John 15:26, which the theologians who produced the creed held to be the central biblical statement about the origination of the Holy Spirit.

This remains the position of the Orthodox Churches who see the Father as in his own person the sole source and origin of both his Son and his Spirit. It is not that he produced them in time, so that at one point in time there was only the Father but at a later point in time there were the Son and the Spirit as well. All the divine persons are eternal; none of them comes into being in time as creatures do. To say that the Son is eternally begotten of the Father and that the Spirit proceeds from the Father is equivalent to saying that only the Father has his being from and in himself. The Son and the Spirit have a divinity that is not their own but is derived from his. Although they are eternal, divine persons and not creatures who come into being in time, they owe their being to the Father and not to themselves; he has primacy and priority over them. 'The Father is greater than I' (John 14:28).

So, on this approach there is an original underived deity that belongs to the Father alone and there is a derived, dependent deity that the Son and Spirit have because it comes to them from the Father. To put the matter diagramatically may help to make it clear.

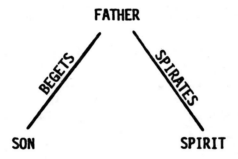

Figure Two

Here the Father is the common source of both the Son and the Spirit. As Irenaeus, a very early theologian, put it: the Son and the Spirit are the two hands of God. Son and Spirit have it in common that they both derive from the Father. They differ from each other because they are related to the Father in different ways. The Son is 'begotten' by the Father; the Spirit 'proceeds' from the Father. The Father 'begets' the Son but 'spirates' (i.e. breathes out) the Spirit. The early fathers kept saying that the difference between begetting the Son and breathing the Spirit was so mysterious that it could not be grasped or explained. Nevertheless, it is an important distinction. You must not say that the Spirit is begotten, because then the Father would have two Sons! In the same way you must not say that the Son is breathed out, because then the Father would have two Spirits!

What perhaps they were getting at, in using these two different verbs to describe how Son and Spirit derive from the Father, is that the coming forth of the Son is like a human begetting, in that it results in the production of another centre of personal life who is of the same 'stuff' as his Father, but who stands over against him as a second person distinct from him. They are one in their deity; yet, like any parent and child, they are sufficiently distinct for the one to love and be loved by the other.

On the other hand the coming forth of the Spirit from the Father is more like the production of a divine breath that carries within itself God's being, life, truth and power. In the Son the Father finds a partner for his love and in the Spirit he finds a way of communicating that love first to the Son and then to us. The Son is the primary *object* of the Father's love: it makes good New Testament sense to say 'The Father loves the Son' (John 5:20). However, there is no equivalent statement that 'The Father loves the Spirit,' for that would be an inappropriate thing to say. The Spirit is not the personal *object* of the Father's love, but rather its personal *communication*. The special relationship of the Spirit to the Father's love is expressed in Romans 5:3: 'God has poured out his love into our hearts by the Holy Spirit whom he has given us.' The difference between the begetting of the Son and the breathing out of the Spirit has something to do with the difference between originating someone to love and originating someone else by whom that love can be conveyed.

The implications of all that for understanding how the Spirit is a distinct divine person we shall discuss further in the next chapter. Meanwhile we resume our exposition of the eastern Orthodox position by emphasising again that central to it is the insistence that the Father alone is the source and origin of both the Son and the Spirit. In regard to the Spirit, although the Orthodox have never altered the credal phrase, 'who proceeds from the Father,' and have indeed consistently protested against the western addition of the words 'and from the Son' (in Latin *filioque*), they have in practice interpreted the creed to mean 'who proceeds from the Father *alone*.' As the Father is the sole begetter of his Son, so he is the sole breather out of his Spirit.

When we measure this eastern Orthodox understanding of the origin of the Spirit from the Father by the scriptural teaching that it seeks to elucidate and interpret, we shall see that it has both a great strength and a great weakness.

Its great strength is its unambiguous affirmation of the priority of the Father over both the Son and the Spirit. All three partake of the one divine being and nature; the Father is first as the source and origin of the other two. This is a faithful transcription into the language of later theology of what the New Testament clearly proclaims. Although Paul and John ascribe to the Son the divine name *Kurios*, Lord, and although the divinity of the Spirit is as clearly implied, the title *Theos*, God, belongs in a special way to the Father. It is used only occasionally of the Son and not at all of the Spirit. Although the Son is 'in the form of God' (Phil 2:6 RSV) and the Word who is God (John 1:1), nevertheless 'the Son can do nothing by himself; he can do only what he sees his Father doing' (John 5:19). His purpose is not simply to draw men to himself but to be the one true and living way by which they may come to the Father (John 14:6).

So in Paul if the ascended Jesus is indeed the *Kurios*, at whose name every knee shall bow and every tongue confess, he occupies that position not for his own glory but 'to the glory of God the Father' (Phil 2:9-11). Paul can even envisage the day when, all his work done, the Lord Christ 'hands over the kingdom to God the Father . . . Then the Son himself will be made subject to him who put everything under him, so that God may be all in all' (I Cor 15:24,28).

So in the New Testament the Father is the prime source and the ultimate end of everything that the Son does and is. Within the divine being that they both share, the Father is first and the Son is second. It is true both of his time on earth and from eternity to eternity in heaven that 'the Father and I

are one' (John 10:30) and that 'the Father is greater than I'
(John 14:28).

The same is true of the Spirit. If we turn again to what John
says about the giving of the Spirit, we shall see that even when
the immediate focus of attention is on the Son's part in
sending the Spirit, there is nearly always a reference to the
Father as the ultimate source from whom the Spirit comes.
For example in John 15:26, although the Spirit is sent by the
Son, nevertheless the point of origin is 'from the Father'. In
the other passages we reviewed earlier in this chapter the
Spirit is given in response to the prayer or to the completed
work of the Son; nevertheless it is the Father rather than the
Son who gives him. If it is the Son who baptises with the
Spirit, it is because he himself in his own baptism received the
Spirit from the Father.

To sum up, if the relationships between Father, Son and
Spirit that come to light in the life of the incarnate Son reflect
and reveal the eternal relationships between Father, Son and
Spirit within the life of God, we have every reason to join our
eastern Orthodox brethren in holding that the primary and
most basic thing to say about the Spirit is that 'he proceeds
from the Father.' The New Testament basis for that
statement is clear and sure.

If however the eastern Orthodox position has a great
strength, it has also a great weakness: it does not make
sufficiently clear how the coming of the Spirit is cradled in
and dependent upon the work of the Son. If we look back at
Figure Two, which represents basic eastern trinitarian thinking, we shall see that, while it insists on the dependence of the
Spirit and the Son upon the Father, it says nothing about the
relation of the Son and the Spirit to each other. The third
article of the Nicene creed in its original form, to which the
Orthodox remain committed, does justice to the teaching of
John about the relation of the Spirit to the Father; but, it fails
to do justice to what the same Johannine teaching says about
the relation of the Spirit to the work and person of the Son.

One of the main emphases of Jesus' farewell discourses in
John is on the intimate relationship between the Spirit and
the Son. We have made the point repeatedly and need only

remind ourselves that it is the going away of the Son that enables a new coming of the Spirit (John 16:7); the Spirit himself does nothing independently of the Son for his whole work is to take what is there for us in the Son and communicate it to us on our side of the relationship. In Acts, also, the mission of the Spirit is to enable and empower the message about Jesus (Acts 1:8) and Paul sees the whole purpose of the Spirit as being to transform us into the likeness of Christ (II Cor 3:18).

If the relationship of Son and Spirit in their work on earth is as close and intimate as all these New Testament writers insist, their relationship within the eternal life of God himself must be equally close. If Son and Spirit are the two hands of God, as Irenaeus taught,[2] they are, on all the New Testament evidence, closely clasped hands. It will not do in a credal statement to speak only of the Spirit's relation to the Father and to remain silent about his relation to the Son.

Such a silence can indeed have dangerous practical consequences. If in our thinking we loosen the connection between Christ and the Spirit, we are in danger of severing one of the nerve-centres of the New Testament gospel. If the Son and the Spirit are seen as semi-independent expressions of the divine life of the Father, it might be possible to be in the Spirit without being in the Son and so to have a relationship to God that is not mediated by Jesus, to try to reach the Father by some other spiritual path than the one true and living way he has given.

There is at least the possibility that this has sometimes happened in eastern Orthodoxy. Karl Barth for example suggested that Russian Orthodoxy had a tendency to lapse into a Christless mysticism, just because it did not clearly enough emphasise that the sure sign of being in the Spirit is to confess that Jesus is Lord.[3]

Nearer home there are at the present time both radical theologians and Anglican bishops who would welcome a return to the original eastern form of the creed which emphasises the Spirit's relationship to the Father at the expense of his relationship to the Son. They do so because it opens the door to an accepting attitude to the other world religions, providing a basis for recognising in them a valid spiritual relationship to God that bypasses Jesus. That may be an advantage for those for whom that sort of pluralism is the highest form of religion. Those however who share the New Testament conviction that God's self-revelation in Christ is the one way to salvation and the final touchstone of religious reality will continue to insist that the Holy Spirit is the one who comes from Christ and whose chief work is to bring us to the confession of Christ. In that case the relationship of the Spirit to the Son is very near the heart of what the gospel affirms about the Spirit in a way that the Nicene creed in its original form does not adequately recognise.

Eastern credal reticence about the relationship of the Spirit to Christ can also open the door to the kind of second blessing pentecostalism in which Son and Spirit preside over distinct areas of God's saving activity. I receive salvation from sin from Christ crucified and then, having fulfilled certain conditions, I go on to the second stage which is to be baptised in the Holy Spirit into the fullness of God's life and power.

I discussed the theological inadequacies and pastoral dangers of that position fully in *Reflected Glory*.[4] Suffice it here to say that when the sphere of the Spirit is regarded as independent of Christ, people can very easily run off into a kind of charismania where speaking in tongues or even falling down on the floor become the authenticating hallmarks of life in the Spirit. Dramatic healings and prophecies become the centre of our attention in and for themselves, so that we can forget to ask whether they point to Christ as their source and affirm the priorities that his gospel lays down.

From all this we can perhaps see more clearly that the right relating of the Spirit to the Son is not merely some nicety of trinitarian theology that can be left to those who are skilled and interested in such things. On the contrary it has an important bearing on biblical and pastoral concerns that are at the forefront of Christian attention in our own day. A failure to affirm the strong tie that unites Son and Spirit in the New Testament can lead to a Christless mysticism, a religious pluralism and a charismatic excess, all of which are much in evidence on the contemporary scene. For all these reasons we need to say more about the Spirit-Son relationship than was said by the Nicene creed in its original form.

Eastern theologians would of course be quick to come to the defence of their own position. They would say, from a pastoral and practical point of view, that Christless mysticism, religious pluralism and charismatic excess appear in western Christianity where the creed emphasises the Spirit-Son relationship at least as much as in eastern Christianity where it does not.

Along more theological lines they would protest that their position, properly understood, allows for no separation between what the Son does and what the Spirit does. For them the Son and the Spirit both have a single source in the Father and are 'of one substance', that is, of the same being and nature as the Father, so that there can be no question of any division or separation between them.

They would further argue that the fact that the Spirit has his eternal origin in the Father alone is not in conflict with the other fact that in the history of salvation he works in closest connection with the Son and is sent into the world in new power and presence as a result of the Son's cross and resurrection. It is indeed Jesus who in gospel history sends the Spirit to the disciples, but the Spirit whom he sends is truly the Spirit of God who has his origin in the Father alone.

To this last point the western response would be that it is difficult to maintain both that the Son is so closely connected with the coming of the Spirit at Pentecost and that he has no connection with the origination of the Spirit within the eternal life of God. If God has revealed to us that the Spirit comes from the Son as well as from the Father at Pentecost, is that not a pointer to the fact that always and eternally he comes from the Son as well as from the Father? When God acts in history he shows himself to us as he really and eternally is. One of the things that he reveals to us is the dependence of the Spirit on the Son. Have we, therefore, any right to deny that dependence by saying that in the eternal dimension of God's life the Spirit comes from the Father alone? There must be a correspondence between what God reveals of himself in the gospel and what he eternally is. We must not, therefore, affirm the relationship between the Spirit and Christ in the gospel and deny, ignore or underplay it in the eternal life of God.

To which the eastern Christians would reply again that, although they have not affirmed the relationship of the Spirit to Christ in the creed, they have by no means denied it or ignored it in their teaching. Gregory of Nyssa, the fourth century theologian, who has had a most important influence in shaping Orthodox thinking, says that, although the Spirit is derived from the Father, he is also, 'of the Son'. Indeed we may say that he proceeds from the Father *through* the Son. The Spirit, says Gregory, is like a third candle lighted from a first candle through a second candle.[5] The light has its origin in the first candle (the Father) but it is transmitted to the third candle (the Spirit) through the second candle (the Son). The Spirit has his being from the Father, although he receives that being not directly and immediately but through the Son. We should note this formula 'from the Father through the Son', which has support in eastern theologians like Gregory and, as we shall see later, has great possibilities for reconciling eastern and western Christians by emphasising equally the things that have been most important to each.

Meanwhile we should sum up our estimate of the eastern position. Its strength lies in its strong affirmation of the priority of the Father as the sole ultimate origin of both the Son and the Spirit which is entirely in line with New Testament teaching. Its weakness is that it does not emphasise with the same clarity the relationship that the New Testament equally affirms between the Spirit and the Son.

The Western Position – Both Father and Son Breathe Forth the Spirit

We turn now to the alternative western answer to our

opening question, 'Who gives the Spirit?' Where the eastern Church answers in its form of the creed 'the Father alone', the western Church answers, 'The Father *and the Son*.' In due course the western Church, led by the pope, unilaterally altered the creed to incorporate that answer. It was this papal claim to have the right to alter the creed without the consent of an ecumenical council that caused the Orthodox as much offence as the alteration itself. The controversy between the two has from the start been not just about the theological question as to who gives the Spirit, but also and as much about the authority of popes to alter creeds. That aspect of the controversy is not directly relevant to us here, but it has always been important and has unhappily roused much passion and bitterness on both sides.

So ultimately in the West, under the all-pervasive influence of the thinking of St Augustine of Hippo who here, as in so much else, is the dominating western theological figure, the third article of the Nicene creed was altered to read, 'I believe in the Holy Spirit, the Lord, the giver of life, who proceeds from the Father *and the Son*'. The Latin for 'and the Son' is *Filioque*, so that the whole discussion has been called the *Filioque* controversy.

Augustine and the western Church after him were less concerned about the priority of the Father than they were about the equal deity of the Son. The Arian heresy had denied Christ's eternal divinity and it was a main concern of western teaching to emphasise that the Son as much as the Father is an equal sharer in the one divine being and nature. Since the Son is as much God as the Father, argues Augustine[6], he is as much involved as the Father in the origination of the third divine person, the Holy Spirit.

In the East to originate other divine persons was seen as the sole prerogative of the Father: in the West to originate the divine person of the Spirit was seen as the prerogative of the divine nature which Father and Son both share. So the Spirit was declared to proceed from the Father and the Son. This was taught first by Augustine at the turn of the fourth into the fifth century and then by the theologians who followed him. By the eleventh century it had become the accepted western position, so that it was added to the creed of the church of Rome and then inevitably to the creeds of all the churches that owed allegiance to Rome. As we have already seen it was left untouched by the Churches of the Reformation which were content to espouse the traditional western position on this matter.

The introduction of this new clause into the creed led, with a horrible inevitability, to the first great schism in the Church between the Orthodox of the East and the Catholics of the West. They broke communion with each other about who gave the Spirit and who could alter the creed. Only in our own time have living and constructive contact and discussion been resumed between them. Reconciliation will require that the two sides who could not do justice to what was important to each other then should do so now. We are, therefore, discussing a matter that is not only of great theological and pastoral concern but has important ecumenical implications. However, before we look at possibilities of reconciliation between these two great Christian traditions we should subject the western position to the same critical examination that we have already applied to the eastern and ask once more where its strengths and its weaknesses lie.

First, however, it will help us to grasp and explicate the western position, and the way it understands the trinitarian relationships of Father, Son and Holy Spirit if we again lay it out in diagram form.

Looking at this figure we can see the characteristic features of the western position which constitute its strengths and its weaknesses over against the eastern churches. We note that:

1. The Father alone begets the Son, but the Father and the Son together breathe out the Spirit, acting 'as one principle and in a single act' to quote the formula used by Augustine and echoed by the Catholic medieval theologians. So the Spirit does indeed proceed from the Father and the Son, which really means from the one divine being and nature that Father and Son share.

2. To this Augustine added that the Father was the *principle* source of the Spirit, because ultimately it is from him alone that both Son and Spirit come, as our diagram

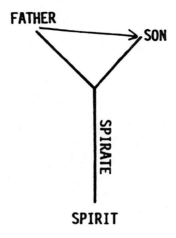

Figure Three

makes clear. The Spirit comes from the Father both directly and indirectly through the Son, because the Son himself has his origin in the Father. This also our diagram makes clear.

So in its own way the western tradition in its original form recognises, even if it does not underline, the priority of the Father in bringing forth both the Son and the Spirit. We have already seen how the East in turn started off by recognising without emphasising the part of the Son in sending the Spirit. So, at least in their early stages, the two traditions each took into account what was important to the other. This suggests that at the beginning the theological gulf between them was not as unbridgeable as later, after centuries of separation, it came to seem. It is only fair to add that in later developments in the West after Augustine the priority of the Father, though never denied, fell into the background and was given scant attention.

3. The strength of the western credal claim that the Son has a central part to play in the giving of the Spirit is that it accurately reflects what the relevant scriptural passages say. If the Paraclete passages in John make it clear that the Father is the primary source of the Spirit - the eastern emphasis --

they make it equally clear that the Spirit is sent by the Son – the western emphasis.

We need only recall such passages as John 15:26 which speaks of 'the Counsellor whom I will send to you from the Father,' and John 16:7, 'If I go I will send him to you', and also the risen Jesus breathing upon his disciples and saying, 'Receive the Holy Spirit' (John 20:22). To such passages the West appeals for biblical backing and such an appeal is fully justified. The western emphasis on the strong relation between the Spirit and the Son is part of the gospel as given and is needed as bulwark against the Christless mysticism, religious pluralism and charismatic excess which can easily intrude when we try to enter into life in the Spirit as something apart from life in the Son.

The trouble with the *filioque* clause is that, although it rightly draws attention to the dependence of the Spirit on the Son, it does not at the same time affirm the dependence of the Son on the Spirit (e.g. in his birth and baptism) and does not make clear the priority of the Father over both Son and Spirit. The Spirit does come from the Son but not in the same way that he comes from the Father; it will not do to name Father and Son together as though they played the same part in the coming of the Spirit. The East is in harmony with Scripture when it insists that his ultimate origin is in the Father alone. The question is how we can express both the primacy of the Father and the participation of the Son.

4. The chief weakness of the western position is that it involves a downgrading of the Holy Spirit in comparison with the Son. If we glance again at the diagram we shall see that the persons of the Trinity are at different levels in a kind of divine hierarchy. The Father originates the Son and the Spirit and is himself originated by neither. The Son is originated by the Father and has an equal share with the Father in originating the Spirit. The Holy Spirit is reduced to an inferior position, because he is originated by the Father and the Son but himself has no part in the origination of any divine person.

For Augustine, as we have already seen, an attribute of the divine nature is that it produces divine persons. For the Son to be fully divine he must with the Father have a part in bringing forth the Spirit. If, however, in the Augustinian scheme, the Spirit has no part in producing any divine person, then we must ask whether the Spirit is really divine at all. The Son exercises the divine prerogative in regard to the Spirit which the Spirit does not exercise in regard to the Son. Within the divine life the Son is creative in a way that the Spirit is not. The Son shares in bringing forth the Spirit, but the Spirit has no share in bringing forth the Son.

For the East the Father in his own person originates both the Son and the Spirit, so that these two are on exactly the same level in both owing their being to him. The East has always protested that the trinitarianism of the West as expressed in the *filioque* clause of the creed involves a subordination and depression of the Holy Spirit over against the Son, so that the West has never been able to do full justice to the distinctive contribution that the Holy Spirit makes to our salvation. Attention is so concentrated on Christ that the Spirit and his work can be neglected and sometimes almost forgotten.

Eastern theologians have not been slow to point out that this neglect of the Spirit which is involved in western trinitarianism is theologically out of tune with the New Testament gospel and has had dire practical effects in western Christianity. It is possible to be Christ-centred in a way that stops you from being open to the Spirit, so that the Spirit can be seen not as a distinct divine person to be worshipped and glorified along with the Father and the Son, but so swallowed up into Christ that the work of the Spirit can be seen simply as the mode of action of the ascended Jesus. Berkhof's proposal to reduce the three persons to two, which we discussed at length earlier, can now be seen more clearly as simply carrying through to its logical conclusion the western tendency to depreciate the Spirit in favour of the Son which has been present since Augustine.

From this point of view we can understand the pentecostal movement as a protest against the exclusive Jesus-centredness of western Christianity in both its Protestant and Catholic forms. The Pentecostals have taught us all afresh that as well as the fixed point of what Christ has done for us once and for all, there is the spontaneous liberating action of the Spirit with all the enthusiasm, expectation and openness that it brings. The givenness of the Word has to be set in the context of the livingness of the unpredictable Spirit. The deed done on Calvary long ago has its contemporary effect in the present inrushing of pentecostal power.

The eastern accusation against the West on this point is expressed in a more sober manner by Kallistos Ware, who started life an Anglican but is now an Orthodox bishop. He says: 'The Latins, while affirming the divinity of the Spirit, have failed to appreciate sufficiently his distinct personality. As a result of the *filioque* they have tended to treat the Spirit as a function and instrument of the Son, and not as a sovereign and co-equal *hypostasis* [person] in his own right. This has meant that inadequate attention is paid in western theology to the work of the Spirit, in the world, in the life of the Church and in the daily experience of each Christian. The living and immediate presence of the Spirit has been too much forgotten, and so the Pope has come to be regarded as the vicar of an absent Christ, while the Church has come to be understood predominantly in terms of earthly power and jurisdiction and not in terms of divine grace and of a free and direct encounter with God in the Spirit'.[7]

That is a temperate statement of the Orthodox case, when compared with, for example, that of Vladimir Lossky who traces every weakness in western Christianity to the depreci-ation of the Spirit which, according to him, acceptance of the *filioque* involves. Alasdair Heron summarises these accusa-tions as follows. Western trinitarianism involves 'a sub-ordination of the Holy Spirit to the person of Jesus Christ which tends towards a "depersonalisation" of the Spirit, a reduction of him to a mere "power" flowing from Christ, and so loses sight of his sovereign freedom and initiative as the Spirit, who like the Word, is one of what Irenaeus called "the two hands of God". No longer does "he blow where he wills"; rather "it goes where it is sent"'.[8]

Where the Spirit does not have his rightful place, authori-tarianism easily creeps in where all the emphasis is upon the

given word of an infallible Bible on the Protestant side, or of
an infallible Pope on the Catholic side. When that happens,
our need to see and confess the truth of the gospel for
ourselves can easily recede into the shadows. In worship this
can lead to the rigidity of a fixed liturgy or the even greater
rigidity of a minister-dominated free church service, where
the freedom of the Spirit to act spontaneously among and
through the congregation is cramped and diminished.

To quote Heron again, the western position has led to 'an
unbalanced emphasis on the "objective" rather than the
"subjective", on the "given" rather than on "the yet to be
received", on established and settled authority, whether of
Church or of Bible, rather than creative freedom in the Spirit,
on the past rather than on the future and even on rational
understanding, focussed upon the Word made flesh, rather
than upon personal engagement on the living pilgrimage of
faith, hope and love in the power of the transforming Spirit.'[9]

Western Christians of nearly all denominations will at
once protest that these accusations are unfairly one-sided
and exaggerated. On calm reflection they will come to see
that they are often uncomfortably near the mark for both
western Catholicism and Protestantism in their traditional
forms. It was precisely such defects in the western Churches
that led to the protest of liberalism on behalf of the freedom
of the spirit of man, and of pietism and later pentecostalism
on behalf of the freedom of the Spirit of God. The
subordination of the Holy Spirit to the Son in western
Christendom is by no means confined to the exotic
technicalities of trinitarian theology, but goes on manifesting
itself in all sorts of ways in the life and worship of the
Churches.

So our resumed debate with the Orthodox has to do not
just with reaching agreement in a disputed clause in the creed,
but with the recovery on both sides of a Christian lifestyle
that is properly related both to the once-and-for-all action of
God in Christ, that gives the Church its foundation and its
norm, and also to the action of the Spirit who gives the
Church the same access to the divine freedom and creativity
that he gave to Jesus in his baptism. Our whole Christian

existence like our worship of the Father is to be 'in Spirit and in truth' (John 4:24). We are to live in the freedom of the Spirit, so that we can say our own 'Yes' and thus glorify the Son. We are also to live in the once-given truth of the gospel, in living conformity to and continuity with what God has revealed to us and done for us in the incarnation, death and resurrection of Jesus Christ.

In the West the givenness of the gospel, and of the Bible and the Church as the communicators of the gospel, have tended to stifle and sometimes even quench the freedom of the Spirit in most of the main-line Churches. When revivalist movements have arisen to proclaim and practise the freedom of the Spirit, they have tended in over-reaction to sit loose to the christological centre and run off into different forms of extremism and even chaos. Conformity to Christ and freedom in the Spirit have appeared as opposing alternatives rather than two sides of the same Christian coin, each depending upon and leading back to the other.

This means that the one-sided domination of the Son over the Spirit that comes to expression in the *filioque* clause needs to be corrected by a trinitarian approach that sees Son and Spirit as interdependent persons who together initiate us into the fullness of life that the Father has for us. Renewed contact with the Orthodox East is most likely to be a factor of major importance in helping this to happen, even if we have to remind such as Lossky that dead institutionalism is by no means the sole prerogative of the West or a poisoned product of the *filioque*, but can be found in the Churches of the East as well.

In neither case is a right theology of Son and Spirit an automatic guarantee of a right relationship with either Son or Spirit. A good map will not by itself get you where you should be, but it will point you in the right direction. A balanced trinitarianism will not by itself unite our life with God's life although it will help to draw our attention to what God is offering and what we have been missing till now.

Possibilities of Reconciliation and Advance

We have to this point looked at the typical answers of Christian East and West to the question, 'Who gives the Spirit?' and we have tried to evaluate the two answers in terms of the New Testament gospel. We have seen that the one side is strong where the other side is weak. The East is strong and the West is weak in stressing the priority of the Father in the sending forth of the Spirit. The West is strong and the East is weak in stressing the necessary connection between the work and person of the Spirit and the work and person of the Son. The question remains as to how we can combine these strengths in a way that will eliminate these weaknesses.

As far as the credal formula is concerned, it is widely agreed in both East and West that we should in the first place go back to the last credal formulation that both sides accepted, namely the Nicene creed without the *filioque*. That is where we parted company and that is where we must resume our common journey. Some western Churches have already taken steps to remove the *filioque*, and others are contemplating such a step. Readers of this book who are present or prospective members of church synods and assemblies may well find that before too long they have to make up their minds on such a proposal. That is why it is so important to be aware of what the issues involved really are. Further it would also be agreed that, as we ourselves have pointed out more than once, the Nicene Creed is inadequate in what it says about the work of the Spirit in general and in particular in what it says about his relation to the Son. The question therefore arises: If both 'He proceeds from the Father' and 'He proceeds from the Father and the Son', are, for the reasons we have discussed, both unsatisfactory what are we to say instead?

Several complicated proposals have been made for new credal statements[10], many of which rule themselves out by their excessive sophistication. I would be in favour of a change that is minimal in form but of major significance in the light of our discussion. I would recommend that the

Churches agree to alter the present western formula by one word and say 'I believe in the Holy Spirit ... who proceeds from the Father *through* the Son.'

Such a formula is, as we have seen, not unknown to the Orthodox, because it is already used by patristic writers of the very highest reputation, notably Gregory of Nyssa in the fourth century. Its theological merits are that it makes unambiguously clear, as the East rightly requires, that the ultimate origin of the Spirit is the Father – 'proceeds *from* the Father' – and at the same time it emphasises what has always mattered in the West, that there is the closest connection between the coming of the Spirit and the coming of the Son – 'proceeds ... *through* the Son.'

It thus does justice not only to the main planks in the trinitarian platforms of the two conflicting traditions, but, even more important, to the two main emphases in what John's gospel says about the coming of the Paraclete. The Father is the sole primary source of the Spirit, as he is the sole primary source of the Son and of everything else that comes to us in creation and redemption. That is his personal prerogative as Father. The Spirit is who he is and does what he does in virtue of the being that he shares with the Son. It is, therefore, through the work of the Son and to glorify the Son that he is sent to us, to remake our humanity in the likeness of the humanity of Jesus.

Those who have heard Michael Ramsey, the former Archbishop of Canterbury, speak on this subject will remember how he tried to get the essential point over. If you stand in King's Cross railway station in London, he would say, to watch the arrival of the Scottish express, you may either say, 'This train comes from Edinburgh *and* York', or you may say, 'This train comes from Edinburgh *through* York.' In both cases the train's journey is clearly defined in relation to these two cities, but in the second case it is much more explicit that the train started not in York but in Edinburgh.

So the formula '*from* the Father *through* the Son' takes full account of the eastern emphasis on the priority of the Father as the source of the Spirit in a way that the present *filioque* clause does not. At the same time it makes it clear, as western teaching requires, that the ministry and person of the Spirit are in the closest possible relation to the ministry and person of the Son. It thus makes the affirmations that the two traditions most want to make, and at least gives promise of holding them both together, as they are held together in the witness of the New Testament. For that reason it might eventually win acceptance in both East and West.

We shall perhaps see more clearly the point that we have now reached with the help of another diagram. This is how the trinitarian relationships look if we say that the Spirit comes from the Father through the Son.

FATHER

SON

SPIRIT

Figure Four

Here in contrast to Figure Three, which represented the classical western position, the priority of the Father over the Son is quite clear, so that part of the eastern objection is fully met. The Spirit does what he does and is who he is because he is sent from the Father through the Son in order that he may lead us through the Son to the Father. There is an outward movement from the Father through the Son to us and there is an inward movement in the Spirit through the Son to the Father.

Also, if the relationships of Father, Son and Spirit within the life of God correspond to their relationships as revealed in the gospel, then we may say that the Spirit has his being in a movement of self-giving that begins with the Father, moves to the Son and from the Son returns to the Father. The Father is the source and the destination of that movement and the Son is at the centre of it, so that we can describe it by saying that the Spirit proceeds from the Father through the Son. We shall explore this more fully in the next chapter.

A further eastern objection has still to be faced. A glance at the diagram will show that the Spirit is still in an inferior position. The eastern objection to the one-sided sub-ordination of the Spirit to the Son, with all its consequences in the life of the Church, has still not been met. The Son determines what the Spirit is and does, but there is no indication that the Spirit also determines what the Son is and does.

We need to recall our argument in chapters three and four how the New Testament itself presents the Son-Spirit relationship. It is not enough to say that the Son imparts to the Spirit what he has received from the Father. That is indeed one side of the matter and it is well represented in Figure Four above. 'He will take what is mine and declare it to you' (John 16:15). As we saw, for the New Testament there is another side to the matter. In the birth of Jesus the Son receives the humanity in which he is incarnate through the action of the Spirit in the womb of Mary at the behest of the Father. In his baptism, which for all four evangelists is one of the great revelatory events of his earthly life, the Son is anointed with his Father's life and power, which are conveyed to him through the action of the Holy Spirit. In his resurrection the Son is given his new 'spiritual body' which is the fulfilment of his and our humanity through the action of the Holy Spirit (I Cor 15:45). So the Son in his incarnation, in birth, baptism and resurrection does what he does and is who he is in virtue of the Spirit's action upon him.

If, then, we are to be true to the total New Testament

witness on this matter, we must say not only that the Spirit comes from the Father through the Son, but also that the Son comes from the Father through the Spirit. There is not just a one-sided dependence of the Spirit on the Son, as the West has taught, but a mutual dependence of the two upon each other. Both have their source in the Father, but each does what he does and is who he is in relation to and dependence upon the other. Their relationship is described better as a co-ordination of the two than as a subordination of the one to the other.

Further, if the relationship between the Spirit and the incarnate Son in the gospel authentically reveals the relationship of the Spirit and the eternal Son in the life of God, there may well be a good case for proposing yet another alteration in the Nicene creed. If in the third article we say that the Spirit 'proceeds from the Father through the Son,' should we not also in the second article say that the Son is 'eternally begotten of the Father *through the Spirit*?' This would have the merit of indicating in the creed the mutual dependence between Son and Spirit that we have discovered in the New Testament and in the trinitarian relationships that are implicit in the good news of Jesus that the gospel proclaims.

We may sum up the position we have now reached in a final diagram that will incorporate all these points.

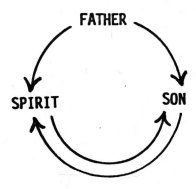

Figure Five

Here the primacy of the Father is still quite clear. From the Father there originate two converging movements of divine self-giving. On the one hand the Son comes from the Father through the Spirit: on the other the Spirit comes from the Father through the Son. The Father sends the Son into the world through the Spirit to fulfil his unique mission, to live, die and rise again for our salvation. Equally the Father sends the Spirit into the world to fulfil his unique mission, to come to our side of the relationship so that we may glorify the Father by confessing the Son with our lips and with our lives. Through the Son we receive the Spirit, and through the Spirit we receive the Son – all to the glory of the Father. From him everything comes, to him everything is to return.

Here we affirm the priority of the Father and the mutual dependence of the Spirit and the Son. The two hands of God are clasped in the closest embrace of mutual support and cooperation before they are stretched out to gather in the world. The Son in his work and his person is from the Father through the Spirit: the Spirit in his work and person is from the Father through the Son. To be rightly open to the Father is to be faithful to the Son in the Spirit, and to be free in the Spirit through the Son.

We started with the question, Who gives the Spirit? We have answered, with the help of East and West, The Father through the Son. And as we have looked at what is involved in the debate about the *filioque,* we have also found ourselves asking, Who gives the Son? and answering, The Father in the power of the Spirit.

Notes on Chapter Five

(1) Our purpose in this chapter is not to trace either the complicated history or the detailed development of the so-called *Filioque* controversy, but simply to indicate and discuss some of the salient differences between the approaches of the eastern and western Churches. Those looking for a more extended treatment are referred in the first place to the volume of papers produced by the World

Council of Churches, *Spirit of God, Spirit of Christ*, Geneva/ London, WCC and SPCK, 1981. The first chapter traces the history of the controversy; subsequent chapters suggest from different contemporary denominational perspectives ways in which it might be resolved.
Other useful works on the subject include:
E.J. Fortman, *The Triune God*, London, Hutchinson, 1972 ad loc.; George S. Hendry, *The Holy Spirit in Christian Theology*, London, SCM Press, 1957, pp 36-52;
H. Kung and J. Moltmann (ed) *Conflicts about the Holy Spirit, Concilium* 128, 1979;
E.L. Mascall, *The Triune God*, Worthing, Churchman Publishing, 1986, Chapter V; and
P. Toon and J. Spiceland (ed) *One God in Trinity*, London, Samuel Bagster, 1980, pp 62-70.

(2) Irenaeus, *Against Heresies*, Book 2, Chapter 1, Para 1.
(3) Karl Barth, *Church Dogmatics*, I:1 (second Edition), Edinburgh, T. & T. Clark, 1975, p 481.
(4) See especially *Reflected Glory*, chapter 3, pp 37-50.
(5) Gregory of Nyssa, 'On the Holy Spirit' in *A Select Library of Nicene and Post-Nicene Fathers*, Vol 5, Schaff and Wade ed, Grand Rapids, Michigan, Eerdmans, 1979, p 317.
(6) Augustine of Hippo 'On the Trinity' Book 15, Para 47 in *A Select Library of Nicene and Post-Nicene Fathers*, Vol 3, Schaff and Wade ed, Grand Rapids, Michigan, Eerdmans, 1980, p 225.
(7) Kallistos Ware in *A History of Christian Doctrine*, H. Cunliffe-Jones ed. Edinburgh, T. & T. Clark, 1978, p 211.
(8) Alasdair Heron, 'The *filioque* in recent Reformed theology' in *Spirit of God, Spirit of Christ*, Lucas Vischer ed, Geneva, WCC, 1981, p 113.
(9) A. Heron, *ibid*, p 144.
(10) For example J. Moltmann who wants us to profess faith in 'The Holy Spirit, who proceeds from the Father of the Son, and who receives his form from the Father and the Son', See J. Moltmann *The Trinity and the Kingdom of God*, S.C.M., London, 1981, p 187.

Chapter Six

The Giving in God

In this chapter we have to ask again the basic question that
has been with us throughout the book: Who is the Holy
Spirit? This time we have to ask it in its most fundamental
form. We have already asked, 'Who is the Holy Spirit in
relation to the Christian community?', and 'Who is the Holy
Spirit in relation to the incarnate Christ?' Now we must ask,
'Who is the Holy Spirit in the eternal life of God himself?'

At first sight it may seem a very arrogant question. Who
are we to probe into the mysteries of the divine being? Is it not
enough to believe the gospel as it has been given to us? In it we
have been shown all we need to know and we have no means
of knowing any more. To look into the secrets of God's own
life can only end by dazzling and blinding ourselves with an
intensity of divine light that our creaturely nature cannot
cope with. Such an enterprise can only distract us from the
task of proclaiming and living out the good news that we
have been given.

Such demurrings need to be taken seriously. There is a way
of theorising and speculating about God that is both
arrogant and irrelevant to the life of the Christian community. We would do well to come to terms with one of the
central themes of eastern Orthodox theology, that at best we
can say only what God is not, but never what he is. Wrong
thoughts and words about him can make it impossible for us
to find him; even the profoundest and most orthodox
thoughts and words can never contain him or explain him –
only point us towards him. He can be known in the end only

by being loved and worshipped, not by being defined or understood. We have to keep this in mind if we dare to say anything about the trinitarian relationships that constitute God's own life. Here is mystery beyond our penetrating, and glory beyond our comprehending. In the end we are left to exclaim with St Paul: 'Oh the depths of the riches of the wisdom and knowledge of God! How unsearchable his judgments, and his paths beyond tracing out!' (Rom 11:33).

Why then pursue our question at all? Why not keep a reverent and adoring silence? Why not be content with knowing who the Holy Spirit is for us without enquiring who he is for God? If it were simply a matter of satisfying our soaring curiosity, then silence would best befit us here. The only reason for speaking about God as he is, is that the gospel is about knowing God as he is. The gospel offers us not just a knowledge of our own situation and of God's gracious and abundant provision for us, but a knowledge of God himself. It is not a matter of our storming the heavens to invade his secrets. Rather he himself has come into our human world and shown himself to us and invited us to know him as he eternally is. For if the gospel does not show us God as he really and eternally is, then it is a deception and not the truth, a concealment and not a revelation.

Especially in John's gospel, it is emphasised again and again that at the heart of the eternal life that Jesus brought is a knowledge of God as he really is. When Philip asks Jesus, 'Lord show us the Father', he is rebuked not for arrogance but for ignorance: 'Anyone who has seen me has seen the Father' (John 14:8-9). Through Jesus Christ we see into the hidden heart of God. Jesus himself prayed: 'Now this is eternal life: that they may know you the only true God, and Jesus Christ, whom you have sent' (John 17:3). To be a Christian is not simply to be rescued and renewed by him, nor is it only to proclaim and serve him: it is to know him as he is. It is to adore him both for what he does for us and for what he shows himself to be as he does it. We come to realise that the reason he loves us is that in himself he *is* love (I John 4:16).

Such knowledge is, of course, not cold or theoretical. We do not analyse God as we analyse a scientific specimen. We know him because in Christ and by his Spirit he has brought us into relationship with himself. Our knowledge of God most nearly resembles the knowledge one person has of another who loves him. It is a knowledge that stands in awe before his mysterious, holy, otherness and yet at the same time rejoices in all of himself that he has revealed to us by which we are able to worship him with our whole heart and mind.

In the gospel God has given himself to be known as Father, Son and Holy Spirit. In what he does for us in Christ, we have access to the Father through the Son and in the Spirit. We are intimately related to each of them in a way that is appropriate to each of them. That is why we are justified in pressing on with our question, Who is the Holy Spirit in the life of God? It is not at all that we want to go beyond what he has revealed. It is precisely because in the gospel God has revealed himself, and given us highly significant clues as to how the three persons who are related to us are also related to one another. So our question may be more accurately rephrased: What can we learn from what the Spirit is and does in Christ, about what he is and does in the eternal life of God?

Having justified the question, let us now see what can be done towards answering it. From what we know in the gospel and from our own experience of what the Spirit does, what can we say about who the Spirit is? We may make several points:

1. *In the eternal life of God the Spirit is a centre and source of personal activity distinct from the Father and the Son, although in the closest relationship to them.* In other words the Spirit is related to the Father and the Son as one person to two other persons. He shares their being but he also has personal relationships with them. He is not just the way in which they act, as Berkhof suggested, but a person who initiates and executes actions of his own, which are distinct from the acts both of the Father and the Son.

In the accounts of the baptism of Jesus in Matthew and Luke it is not entirely clear whether what descended on Jesus is being thought of as an impersonal something called holy spirit, or as a personal someone whose name is the Holy

Spirit. Later, when the same Spirit comes upon the Church
on and after the day of Pentecost, that event is presented by
both Luke and John as the coming of another person distinct
from Jesus. In Luke the going away of Jesus is the signal for
the coming of this other, whose connection with Jesus as well
as his distinction from Jesus are both indicated by saying that
Jesus sends him. His connection with and distinction from
the Father are likewise indicated by saying that the Father
sends him.

In John the Spirit is the *allos paraklētos* (other advocate)
of the same kind as Jesus, distinct from him in his personal
otherness and in the fact that he serves Jesus by glorifying
him.

Subordination

It is, therefore, entirely legitimate to read the accounts of
the baptism of Jesus given by Luke and John in the light of
the identification of the Spirit as distinct person which these
same two gospel writers make later. We can then speak of the
Father in person sending the Spirit in person upon the Son in
person. The Spirit is the giving Gift whom the Father bestows
to be the inseparable companion of the eternal Son in the
whole course of his incarnate life. Occasionally his presence
with and in the Son is acknowledged: most of the time it is
hidden and faceless. Yet from his birth through his baptism
to his resurrection he is always there, renewing, empowering,
transforming the humanity which the Son bears.

What he later is to us as God's adopted children, he first is
to the eternal Son incarnate in Jesus. He is the one on whom,
according to John 1:33, the Spirit comes down and remains.
In his whole human existence he has with him, as the Gift of
his Father, the *paraklētos*, the one whose calling it is to be in
the most intimate way with him. The Spirit is sent by the
Father to the Son; he crosses from one side of the
relationship between Father and Son to the other. He is in
person the presence of the Father on the Son's side of the
relationship. The divinity of the Son is to be understood in a
fully trinitarian context. He is divine because he lives in a
personal relationship of utter trust and obedience with his
Father. He is divine because in his own person he shares the
divine being and nature. He is divine because he is filled with

the Spirit of God, whom he receives from the Father to be in the very depths of his being his divine companion, counsellor and supplier. Something like this is implied in his words 'The Spirit of the Lord is upon me,' if we interpret them in the light of all that the New Testament tells us about the Spirit and his distinct personhood.

What it was like for Jesus to have the Spirit with him and in him in that sort of way is beyond our imagining. The only clue that we have to it is the presence of the same Spirit on our side of the relationship with the Father and the Son, enabling us to receive what they offer and to give them the glory they are due. Because Jesus is human, the Spirit dwells in him in the same way that he dwells in us, although in unimaginable fullness, as one who is distinct from him and yet who continually communicates God's life and presence to the very heart of his being.

But, because Jesus is the eternal Son made man, in his human story we see being acted out the eternal interplay of Father, Son and Spirit within the life of God. As Father, Son and Spirit relate to one another in the gospel story, so do they relate from eternity to eternity. In the baptism of Jesus the eternal self-giving by which, in the person of the Spirit, the Father gives himself to the Son, is revealed in time and in the context of our humanity. The Spirit whom he gives is of the same being as the Father who gives him. He is personally distinct from the Father, so that he can come from the Father to the Son and dwell in him as his divine companion and Paraclete. In the baptism of the Son, understood in the light of what the New Testament tells us about the personhood of the Spirit, we are shown the characteristic shape of the divine life which consists in the dynamic interchange in loving self-giving of Father, Son and Spirit, the three persons who are one God.

2. To this we must immediately add that *the Spirit is a different sort of person from the Father and the Son*. This is a point made but not elaborated by Alasdair Heron in his important book on the Holy Spirit. He says that 'it is legitimate to describe the Spirit as the "third person"... *provided* it is recognised that each of the three is "person" in

distinctive fashion, as Father, as Son, as Holy Spirit. In particular, the difference and complementarity between the Son and the Spirit should not be effaced. The Spirit is God, but God acting within, directing us, not to himself as Holy Spirit, but to the incarnate Son and, in him, to the Father.'[1]

Heron's main point here, often made by the church fathers in the early centuries, is that the personhood of the Spirit is different from the personhood of the Son, because the way the Spirit is related to the Father is quite different from the way the Son is related to the Father. The Spirit is not a second Son, begotten by the same Father. The Spirit is said rather to 'proceed' from the Father, that is to be related to the Father in a way that is different from the 'begotten' Son. The patristic writers declined to explain this distinction any further, holding that it was utterly mysterious and therefore incapable of explanation.

Heribert Mühlen in *Der Helige Geist als Person* uses language that has its roots in Martin Buber, the modern Jewish philosopher, to help us here. According to Mühlen, the Father-Son relationship is what Buber calls an I-Thou relationship, in which two persons relate to each other at either side of a fully personal relationship. In the trinitarian relation the Father is the First Person, the I, who originates and institutes the relationship by addressing the Son, by uttering the Word. That Son or Word thereby becomes the Second Person, the Thou, at the other side of the relationship. The Son is the Father's personal partner, who shares his being, as any son shares the being of his father, but who is personally distinct from him, as any son is from his father, and therefore is the primary object of his self-giving love. Without this partner, the First Person would be shut up in his own solitariness; without the Son the Father would not be Father. Without the First Person, the Second Person would have no being at all: no Father, no Son.

The Spirit is not a second Thou over against the Father; he is not the Father's second partner alongside the Son. In the New Testament the Father speaks to the Son and the Son speaks to the Father, and the Father loves the Son and the Son in response loves the Father. The New Testament in fact keeps on saying things like this about Father and Son, because it sees them as the partners in an I-Thou relationship.

However, the New Testament does not encourage us to say that the Father speaks to the Spirit and the Spirit speaks to the Father, or that the Father loves the Spirit and the Spirit loves the Father. The Spirit is not the partner whom the Father addresses or the object on whom, within the divine life, he eternally bestows his love. It belongs to the Son and not to the Spirit to be in I-Thou relation to the Father. If the Spirit is person, it is in a quite different way from the Son.

3. *Particularly in the West, under the influence of Augustine, the Spirit has often been thought of as the Gift of love between the Father and the Son.*[2] As one of his ways of explaining how God can be both one and three Augustine appeals to the biblical assertion in I John 4:16 that God is love. Augustine asks how in his own being God can be love. God does not begin to love when he has a created universe to be the object of that love. His love for us is simply the expression of what, before and apart from us, he is in himself. He *is* love. Therefore, for God to be love within his own eternal life, there must be in him one who loves and one who is loved. Love is a relationship that implies at least two partners, unless it is self-love. In God from eternity to eternity there is a Father who loves and a Son who is his beloved, to whom he gives himself in outgoing love.

Yet, if the Father is the eternal Lover and the Son is the eternally Beloved, we face the problem about what place there is for the Holy Spirit, who cannot easily be said either to love or to be loved. Augustine's answer to the problem is ingenious. He says that the relationship described by Love has not just two but three elements in it, the Lover, the Beloved and the Love itself, given by each to the other. This Love between Father and Son he identifies as the Spirit. Both Father and Son are, by nature, Spirit. In their loving they give themselves and what they are to each other; they give the Spirit who is their very self to each other. The Spirit is, therefore, first of all the Father's Gift of himself to his Son and then the answering Gift whereby the Son gives himself to the Father.

So, to say that God is love and that God is Trinity turn out
to be two ways of saying the same thing. The Father is the
eternal Lover, the Son is the eternally Beloved, and the Spirit
is the eternal dynamic movement of self-giving Love between
them, whereby the Father first gives himself to the Son and
the Son in response gives himself to the Father. Father, Son
and Spirit are God's three ways of being love, the initiator of
love, the receiver of love and the love itself that is given and
received. Thus the Holy Spirit is that outgoing dynamic
movement of self-giving that constitutes the life of God, and
that both distinguishes and unites the person of the Father
and the person of the Son. So Augustine describes the Spirit
as *vinculum caritatis,* bond of affection, or *nexus amoris,* tie
of love, between Father and Son, or more simply, as the Gift,
the Father's giving to the Son, the Son's giving to the Father.

We have already noticed the great difficulty and objection
that this approach to the person of the Spirit has to face and
we shall soon return to it. We should first, however, recognise
two great, positive contributions that Augustine's doctrine of
the Spirit makes. First of all, Augustine speaks of God, and
especially of the Spirit, in dynamic and not static terms. God
is not pictured as static perfection engaged in eternal contemplation of his own completeness. The Spirit within the life
of God is a perpetual movement of self-giving love between
the Father and the Son. God is, therefore, Father and Son
who as Lover and Beloved are two, but who are held in unity
by the Spirit of love that the one gives to the other.

It is not hard to understand that, when such a God creates
man in his own image, he should create a diversity of persons,
sharing a common humanity, but endlessly different from
each other in sex, race, history and personality, just as Father
and Son share the one divine nature but are personally
distinct the one from the other: and that his purpose for such
distinct human persons should be for them to find their unity
in self-giving love towards one another, just as Father and
Son affirm their unity in giving themselves to each other in
the Spirit. In the same way it makes sense that, when that
purpose is deflected by sin, which is basically a refusal of self-
giving, such a Father and such a Son should devise a way of

reconciliation for the world in the Son's becoming human and offering himself on behalf of humanity in an act of utter self-giving to the Father on the cross, by which the Spirit of self-giving love is released into the world to remake men in their relationships to God and to one another.

The Augustinian analysis of the biblical statement that God is love as involving the Trinity of loving Father, beloved Son and the Spirit of self-giving holds the whole gospel together. The love that this God is, as Father, Son and Spirit, is the very same love that in Christ both made the world and redeemed it.

In the second place, the Augustinian approach to the triune life of God helps us to see rather more clearly that the Holy Spirit is a different sort of divine person from either the Father or the Son. The Father and the Son are partners at either end of an I-Thou relationship which both distinguishes and unites them. The Spirit is the one who moves perpetually across the relationship from the one to the other. In Rublev's famous ikon, the holy Trinity is depicted as the three men who visited Abraham at the oaks of Mamre (Gen 18:1–15). There Son and Spirit are depicted as two human figures, both facing towards the Father, so that both appear to be his partners in I-Thou relationships. It looks as if the Father has the same sort of relationship with the Spirit as he has with the Son. The ikon gets near depicting the Spirit as a second Son – something that the patristic theologians of both East and West explicitly rejected, as we have seen.

In Augustine's presentation, the Spirit is clearly not understood in that way. He is not one of the persons who are relating to each other, but rather the one in whom and by whom their relationship and their self-giving are effected. As Augustine puts it, he is not lover or beloved, but rather the love between them. In terms of the ikon the Spirit is not a third, seated figure alongside Father and Son. He is rather constantly moving personal living energy passing from the Father to the Son and back again, not establishing an I-Thou relationship of his own with either, but rather constituting the relationship between the other two. He is the life and love of the Father endlessly moving out towards the Son and the life and love of the Son endlessly moving back in responding self-giving to the Father. He is, in Bishop John Taylor's phrase the 'Go-Between God'.[3] He is the personal outgoing of the Father to the Son and of the Son back to the Father. He is the divine movement initiated by the Father towards the Son and reciprocated by the Son towards the Father. If he is personal, it is within that movement that his personhood is constituted and is to be located, so that it is a very different sort of personhood from that of either Father or Son. This, at least, Augustine's approach makes unambiguously clear.

What is not so clear is whether and how the Holy Spirit can be thought of as distinct person at all, if we follow the Augustinian approach. A lover is a person, a beloved is another person, but love is the name of a relationship between them or of the attitude that the one has to the other, not the name of a third person distinct from lover and beloved. Also the terms that Augustine uses to describe the Spirit, *vinculum* (bond), *nexus* (tie), and *donum* (gift), are normally used of things rather than of persons.

Augustine undoubtedly intended to affirm the Holy Spirit as the third trinitarian person; but his way of thinking of the Spirit as the mutual love of Father and Son has always tended towards a depersonalising of the Spirit and a virtual binitarianism in which attention is concentrated upon the Father and the Son. These tendencies have always characterised western Christianity and, as we have seen, are still present in it today.

To sum up, then, our conclusions so far; the Augustinian approach is helpful and in harmony with Scripture in its insistence that, within the life of God, the Spirit is who he is and does what he does *between* the Father and the Son: he is the communicator of the one to the other, the agent of their mutual self-giving. On the other hand, the Augustinian approach is less than helpful in its tendency to dissolve the Spirit into a relationship or an attitude rather than affirm him as distinct person. We may thank Augustine, however, for showing us that the Spirit is not the object of the Father's love like the Son. His personhood does not spring from his being loved. Regrettably Augustine does not tell us clearly where it does spring from.

A Way Forward

To help us forward, we look now at the contribution of
Heribert Mühlen to which I have referred more than once.
Mühlen finds his starting point in the twelfth century
theologian, Richard of St Victor, who was concerned in his
own work on the Trinity to find a way of affirming the
personhood of the Spirit more adequately than did the
Augustinian tradition which he had inherited.[4] Mühlen's
concern is to develop Richard's insights and restate them in
modern terms.

Mühlen points out that an I-Thou relationship is not the
only possible relation between two persons. They can also
relate as We. An 'I' and a 'Thou' are partners at opposite ends
of a relation, but when they become 'We' they are acting
together. So the sentence, A loves B, reflects an I-Thou
relationship between A and B, whereas the sentence, A and B
love C, reflects a situation in which A and B are acting
together as 'We', so that they both stand at the same side of
their relationship with C.

Mühlen applies this to the trinitarian relationships. When
the Father brings forth the Son, the Son is the 'Thou' to the
Father's 'I'. But when Father and Son together bring forth
the Spirit, they act together as 'We': the Spirit has his origin
in their shared love. As Mühlen himself puts it, 'The Father
brings forth the Son as his Thou in order that together with
him, he may bring forth the Holy Spirit'.[5]

Mühlen uses this to explain the difference between saying
that the Son is begotten by the Father and that the Spirit
proceeds from the Father and the Son. The Son is 'begotten'
to be the Father's partner, the 'Thou' to the Father's 'I'. The
Spirit is the product of both Father and Son acting together
as 'We' in their shared love. One of Mühlen's ways of
expressing this is to say that the Spirit is the 'We in person' of
the Father and the Son.

All this becomes considerably more intelligible when

Mühlen explains it by analogy with human relationships with which we are all familiar. Father and Son are, within the life of God, related to each other in a way that is somewhat similar to the relationship of husband and wife in marriage. They are the partners in a loving relationship, the two who are constantly affirming their unity in giving themselves, the one to the other.

Husband and wife, however, are not content just to be partners in a mutual love for each other, but are fulfilled when, in their togetherness, acting as 'We', they produce a child. That child, says Mühlen, in relation to his parents is not 'mine' or 'yours', but 'ours'. He belongs to both of them; he is, in fact, the expression of their love for each other in the form of a third person. That is why the child is so lost if his parents' love dies and the relationship to which he owes his being is dissolved. The child who is born of their love expresses in a fully personal way what they are to each other. To use Mühlen's own terminology, a child is the 'We in person' of his parents' love: he has his being out of their giving of themselves to each other. Intense love between two people does not just unite them in a relationship with each other. It is creative and productive of a third person who owes his being to the love that brought him forth and is himself the personalised expression of it.

This, says Mühlen, offers an analogy which will at least help us to approach the mystery of how the person of the Holy Spirit is related to the mutual love of the Father and the Son. He is 'our Spirit' in that he can be referred to equally well as the Spirit of God or the Spirit of Christ. As the child is the product of the togetherness, the 'we-ness', of husband and wife, so the Holy Spirit is the third person who is produced by the togetherness in love, the 'we-ness' of the Father and the Son.

This analogy has of course to be handled with circumspection and sensitivity and not pushed further than it will go. Mühlen is not saying that the Holy Spirit is the child of the Father and the Son. He is not saying that the Spirit has an independent existence of his own outside his relationship to the Father and the Son, the way that a child grows up to have a life of his own apart from his parents. The sole point of the analogy is to demonstrate that there is a creativity about the intense self-giving of the kind of love that has its source in God. It involves not just the exchange of love between the two persons involved, but the production of a new person as the fruit and expression of that love. Marriage and parenthood are the human expression of that creativity, and Mühlen asks us to consider whether the person of the Holy Spirit cannot helpfully be thought of as the personal product of the self-giving of Father and Son, which is the divine prototype of all creativity.

This involves a much needed correction of the Augustinian tradition at this point. The Spirit is not just another name for the mutual love of Father and Son: he is rather the personal product of that love. 'He is the unity of the Father and the Son in person'.[6] In the self-giving of Father and Son there is involved not just a relationship of love, but a third person, the Spirit, who is the product of that love and its bearer from the one to the other. The love that unites the two produces the third. This is a valid principle in human relationships. If these human relationships mirror divine relationships, then it may well be valid within the life of God as well. Mühlen's approach is a great advance on Augustine, because it clearly affirms the distinct personhood of the Holy Spirit. The Holy Spirit is not just love; he is the personal product and expression of love.

It will not, however, have escaped the notice of the discerning reader that Mühlen's position assumes the validity of the *Filioque*, that the Spirit proceeds from the Father *and the Son*. Put simply what he says is: as a child has his origin in the love of his father and his mother, so the Spirit has his origin in the love of the Father and the Son. In the way he expounds his thesis, Mühlen, as a good western Catholic theologian, lays great stress on the joint and equal action of the Father and the Son in bringing forth the Spirit. He is therefore open to many, if not quite all, the objections against that position discussed in the last chapter.

Thus his teaching about the person of the Spirit is not immediately reconcilable with the conclusion we ourselves reached at the end of that chapter, that the Spirit proceeds from the Father *through* the Son. In particular, Mühlen does not really allow for the reciprocity of relationship between the Spirit and the Son which characterises New Testament teaching. In Mühlen the Son is unambiguously prior to the Spirit and the Spirit is unambiguously subordinate to the Son. He cannot find any place for the insight that the Spirit is involved in the coming forth of the Son just as the Son is involved in the coming forth of the Spirit.

The Spirit as the Self-giving of Father and Son

Nevertheless, we can still deploy Mühlen's valuable insight that the self-giving of one person to another results in the production of a third person who is distinct from both the other two. I would want to say that the being of the Spirit *originates* in the self-giving of the Father to the Son, and is further characterised by the responsive self-giving of the Son to the Father.

It is the Father who originates the Spirit. As he eternally gives being to the Son as the divine partner of his love, so he gives himself to that Son in an intensity of self-giving that brings forth the Spirit as the personalised expression of the Father's love for the Son. As against Mühlen and the western tradition to which at this point he is faithful, the Spirit originates not as the expression of the love of the Father *and* the Son, but rather as the personalised expression of the love of the Father *to* the Son. He is not the child of the togetherness, the 'we-ness' of Father and Son, as Mühlen would have it, but the expression of the all-creative love of the Father as he gives himself to his only-begotten Son. The being of the Spirit, like the being of the Son, has its sole source in the self-giving love of the Father. So we uphold the eastern Orthodox, and, we believe, the New Testament insistence that the Father alone brings forth both the Son and the Spirit, but at the same time affirm Mühlen's insight that, when the Father gives himself to the Son, he does not simply establish a relationship but brings forth a third person.

We can make the same point slightly differently, if we look a little more closely at the key statement, the Father gives himself to the Son. Here there is a giver, the Father, and a recipient, the Son, and a gift: and that Gift is personal, since what the Father gives is not just his love, but himself. The Holy Spirit is therefore the 'self' of the Father, who has moved across the relationship, so that he is now on the Son's side of it. The Spirit is the Gift of the Father's very self to the Son. He has his origin in a movement of love that originates in the Father and goes out to the Son whom he has begotten to be the partner of his love.

The Spirit is of one being with the Father, because it is the Father's own self that he gives when he gives the Spirit. Yet the Spirit is personally distinct from the Father, as the one who is given to the Son and is in the Son is personally distinct from the one who gives and who stands over against the Son. The Spirit is of one being with the Son, because they both have their being from the one Father; he is personally distinct from the Son as the Gift is distinct from the one to whom he is given.

When Jesus says, 'I am not alone for the Father is with me' (John 16:32), he refers not just to the loving and providing presence of the Father in heaven from whom he comes, before whom he lives, to whom he prays in his life and offers himself in his death. As well as his relationship to the Father above him, there is a presence of the Father in him and with him on his side of the relationship, as the companion and strengthener sharing his experience from inside. This is the presence of the Spirit whom the Father sends upon him, who is the Spirit of the Father, and who is yet distinct from the Father, because he is with and in the Son as the Son deals with the Father.

We have to say not only that the Spirit originates in a person-creating movement of love from the Father to the Son, but also that the Spirit is who he is and does what he does in relation also to a responding movement of self-giving from the Son back to the Father. The Father's giving to the Son which originates the Spirit is reciprocated in the Son's giving to the Father. The Spirit is not originated by the Son's giving, because the Son first receives him from the Father. Yet he is characterised by it: he is the Spirit in whom the Son responds in self-giving to the Father.

In other words, to describe the Spirit we have also to analyse the sentence 'The Son in response gives himself to the Father'. The Holy Spirit comes into being as the Father's Gift to the Son, but he becomes who he is as the Son's responsive Gift of himself to the Father. When Jesus says, 'I am in my Father' (John 14:20), he is speaking of the Holy Spirit. The Son is not only distinct from the Father in his own person, within the eternal life of God and incarnate on earth; he is also eternally giving himself to the Father, just as he does on the cross. The personal being of the Holy Spirit has its source in the self-giving of the Father to the Son, and once given to the Son, the Spirit becomes also the personalised self-giving of the Son to the Father.

To put it yet another way, two historical events in the life of Jesus specially correspond to the two movements in the eternal life of God, one of which originates and the other of which defines the Spirit. First of all, in the baptism of Jesus, we see the Spirit as the personalised self-giving of the Father to the Son. The Spirit is the Father as given to the Son; he is the Father taking up his abode on the Son's side of the relationship. He has his origin in that embracing acceptance by the Father of his eternal Son, he is the indwelling of the Father in the Son.[6] In him the Father's love for the Son takes the form of a third person in a way that is far beyond our comprehension but to which we have a clue and a pointer in the way that a husband's love for his wife takes personal form and expression in the child that is born of it. It would therefore make good biblical sense to say in the Creed that the Spirit 'proceeds from the Father to the Son,' making clear that his origin is in the initiative of the Father, but that he is what he is in the movement of the Father's love to the Son.

In the second place, the Spirit is also the Spirit of Calvary, the Spirit of the Son's self-giving to the Father. He is the Spirit of whom John 19:30 says that when his work on the cross was triumphantly completed Jesus 'bowed his head and handed over the Spirit (*paredoken to pneuma*).' He is the

Spirit of whom Hebrews 9:14 says that 'through the eternal Spirit he [Christ] offered himself unblemished to God.' So, the Spirit whom the Son receives from the Father, is also the Spirit of the Son's sacrificial self-giving in response to the Father's love. He is the Son as given back to the Father from whom he came; he is the Son taking up his abode on the Father's side of the relationship. He is the Spirit of the Son's utter surrender to the Father; he is the indwelling of the Son in the Father.[7] The Spirit has his origin in the outward movement of the Father's love out to the Son, but he has his destination in the inward movement of the Son's love back to the Father. Again we speak of things that are far beyond us, to which nevertheless we have a clue and a pointer in our own human imaging of that divine love. The Spirit as given back by the Son to the Father is like the child that a mother lays as the personalised expression of her own self-giving in her husband's arms. Its origin was in his self-giving to her and it now becomes the living expression of her self-giving to him.

Because Father and Son share one divine being and nature, their love for each other can become person in one Holy Spirit, who in his origin is the Spirit of the Father whom he gives to his Son, the eternal partner of his divine life, and within that life becomes the Spirit of the Son in whom he gives himself to the Father. He is not just the relationship of love between the two, but the personal product and expression of that relationship in which the Father initiates and the Son responds to his initiative. He proceeds from the Father to the Son and he returns from the Son to the Father.

Thus, in a way that affirms both the priority of the Father, for which eastern Orthodoxy rightly contends, and the essential involvement of the Son, on which western Christians rightly insist, he is the Spirit of the Father and of the Son. He is the Father's Gift of himself in person to the Son; he is the Son's answering Gift of himself in person to the Father. He is the third Person who originates in the self giving of the first Person to the second, and expresses the responsive self-surrender of the second Person to the first.

It is this Spirit who comes to us. Because he is in himself the personal product of the self-giving of Father and Son within the eternal life of God, he can express that self-giving savingly in human history and experience. The Father who in his Spirit has given himself before all worlds to his eternal Son now gives himself in the same way to his incarnate Son in the context of his human life. He gives himself in his Spirit to his Son first to bring him to human birth at Christmas. He gives himself in another way to the same Son in the same Spirit to anoint him with divine authority in his baptism. He gives himself in a third way to the same Son in the same Spirit to transform him into the *eschatos Adam*, the ultimate Man in his resurrection. In these historical events the Father is doing what he has always done, giving himself in his Spirit to his Son.

In the same way the Son who before all worlds gives himself to the Father as to his source and origin, now in his incarnation gives himself to his Father in the context of his human life. In the Spirit from whom he has his birth he grows into his Father's favour and pledges himself to be about his Father's business (Luke 2:52,49). In the Spirit who comes upon him in his baptism he gives himself in life and death to fulfil his Father's purpose. That purpose is our salvation and it is accomplished in a way that is entirely consonant with the eternal being of God, namely in the giving of the Father to the Son in the Spirit and in the giving of the Son to the Father in the same Spirit. God *is* self-giving and it is when that self-giving becomes human history that fallen humanity is redeemed and renewed.

At Pentecost it is this Spirit of the Father's and the Son's self-giving who is poured out on us. The two who have indwelt each other in that Spirit from all eternity now give themselves in that same Spirit to indwell us. Heribert Mühlen points out how in the upper room discourses in John's gospel the coming of the Spirit, who is seen as personally distinct from the Father and the Son is nevertheless seen as the coming of the Father and the Son to indwell the believing company. In John 14:23, having just promised to ask the Father to give them the *allon parakleton*, the other Paraclete, Jesus promises that he and his Father will come to the disciple who loves and obeys him. 'If anyone loves me and obeys my teaching, my Father will love him and *we will come to him and make our home with him*.'

The coming of the Spirit is itself the coming of the Father and the Son. In the Spirit they give themselves to us. The Spirit is one with them as the personal expression of their giving, the one to the other, but distinct from them, as the Gift is from the Giver. The Spirit who is the personal expression of the eternal togetherness in love of the Father and the Son, becomes the personal expression of their togetherness with us. The Spirit is the Father and the Son on our side of the relationship: in him they give themselves to us.

Paul also speaks of God's indwelling us by the Holy Spirit. In I Corinthians 3:16 he says: 'Don't you know that you are God's temple and that God's Spirit lives in you?' The indwelling of the Spirit is the indwelling of God. But Paul also says that Christ dwells in us. In Ephesians 3:16–17, 'being strengthened with power through the Spirit in your inward being', is the closest possible connection with having 'Christ dwell in your hearts through faith.'

Christians are temples indwelt by the Father and the Son. This indwelling is effected by the Holy Spirit in such a way that the personal relation between them and us is preserved in its integrity. They do not become us and we do not become them. Yet in the Spirit they give themselves across the relationship to us, just as in their own life they give themselves across the Father-Son relationship to each other. The indwelling of the Father and the Son in us is the Holy Spirit, who is their personalised self-giving to us. The Spirit is the originating love of the Father and the responding love of the Son given to us in personal form. The Spirit of the Father and the Son comes to us to enable our reception of and our response to what God has done in Christ.

The Spirit is the Gift of the Father and the Son, given in such a way that the Givers, the Gift himself and the recipients of the Gift are all in their different ways persons in personal relationship with one another. In the Spirit all these divine and human persons give themselves to one another through Christ who is both human and divine. So in the Spirit we begin to live a life that is of the same shape as the life of the triune God himself.

Furthermore, the movement of the Spirit *from* the Father *to* the Son in the eternal life of God is extended to humanity in history, when the same Spirit is given to us *from* the Father *through* the Son. In our presentation of the being and function of the Spirit in the triune life of God we have emphasised both the priority of the Father and the essential involvement of the Son. Both these factors are affirmed in what the New Testament says about the coming of the Spirit to Jesus and to us.

In the baptism of Jesus the Father who from all eternity has given himself to his Son in the Spirit does so again in a particular historical situation. The Son, now incarnate, receives the Spirit from the Father and transmits that Spirit first to his own humanity and then after Pentecost to ours. The formula, from the Father through the Son, is validated in different contexts by the witness of John the Baptist (John 1:32-34), the teaching about the coming of the Paraclete in John 14-16 which we have already examined, and in Peter's Pentecost sermon (Acts 2:33). These passages all affirm that the incarnate Son is the intermediary through whom the Spirit is transmitted from the Father to his people. The Father is the source of the Spirit though the only way to receive the Spirit in his New Testament fullness is through the Son.

Is this Position Biblical?

We cannot claim that what we have been saying in this chapter about the Spirit in the eternal life of God is biblical in the sense that it can be supported by the direct citation of biblical texts. The explicit interest of the New Testament is in the coming of the Spirit to us, so that it does not focus direct attention, as we have been doing, on the relationships of the Spirit to the Father and the Son. We would want to claim, however, that the position we have been outlining in this chapter is biblical in another just as legitimate way.

Its starting point is New Testament teaching about the Spirit. What we have been seeking to do is simply to make explicit what in the New Testament is still to a large extent implicit. We have been proceeding on the principle that, when God comes among us to deliver us by his Son and in his Spirit, the way he acts in human history is an expression of his own eternal being. What he himself is eternally is revealed by his saving acts and particularly in his dealings with his incarnate Son. The relationships between Father, Son and Spirit that come to light in the gospel are the relationships that have eternally held among them within the life of God. Our position is, therefore, biblical in the sense that what we have said about the Spirit in God's life is based upon and in conformity with the revelation of himself that God has given in Christ, to which the New Testament is the primary witness. As in Christ he shows himself to us, so he was from the beginning, is now and ever shall be from eternity to eternity.

God is love: that love is lived out in the dynamic of an eternal divine self-giving, which has its source in the Father. The Father eternally constitutes his Son as the partner and object of his love, and gives himself in love to his Son. The Spirit is the divine person who is produced by the self-giving of the Father to the Son. He is distinct from the Father as the person given is distinct from the person giving. He is distinct from the Son as the person given is from the person receiving. The Spirit who has his origin in the love of the Father for the Son is also the bearer of the responsive love of the Son to the Father. He comes into being as the Father gives himself to his Son, but his being is fulfilled as the Son in love gives himself back to the Father. The Spirit is, therefore, primarily the presence of the Father in the Son and, in response, he is also the presence of the Son in the Father.

Son and Spirit both originate in the Father; the Son is perfected in what he receives from the Spirit and the Spirit is perfected in what he receives from the Son. It is by this Spirit, who is the expression of the love of Father and Son for each other, that the Son is born into the world to be the expression of the Father's love to us. It is by this Spirit, who is sent to us through the incarnate, crucified and risen Son, that the Father and the Son may make their home in us.

All this is mystery and when all our best words are spoken and all our best arguments marshalled, it is a mystery still, so far beyond our comprehending that we draw nearer to it in our worship of the triune God than we ever can in our trinitarian theology. Nevertheless, it is revealed mystery. The eternal, triune, divine life has entered human life in the Father's Son who became man in the power of the Father's Spirit. He is the Word made flesh who takes our human words and our thoughts into his service, and uses them to point us in truth to our God and Father who gives himself to us, because apart from us, in his own being, in his own Son and his own Spirit, he *is* love.

Notes on Chapter Six

(1) Alasdair Heron, *The Holy Spirit*, London, Marshall, Morgan & Scott, 1983, p 176.

(2) For Augustine's teaching that the Holy Spirit is the Gift of Love both to us and within the life of God himself, see his treatise, 'On the Holy Trinity' in *Nicene and Post-Nicene Fathers*, Philip Schaff ed. Grand Rapids, Michigan, Eerdmans, 1980, Vol III, Book XV, pp 215-220.

(3) John V. Taylor, *The Go-Between God*, London, SCM Press, 1972.

(4) Especially in his great treatise on the Trinity. There is no easily accessible English Translation. Those who can cope with the original Latin will find the relevant passages in *Patrologia Latina*, ed J.P. Migne, Paris, 1856-66, Vol 196, pp 887-992.
     Those whose curiosity or competence does not extend that far will find accounts of Richard's position in the following:
     Edmund J. Fortman, *The Triune God*, London, Hutchinson, 1972, pp 191-4.
     C.B. Kaiser, *The Doctrine of God*, London, Marshall, Morgan & Scott, 1982, pp 88-9.

(5) Heribert Mühlen, *Der Heilige Geist als Person*, Münster, Verlag Aschendorff, 1963, p 154, English translation mine.

(6) Mühlen, *ibid.* p 166.

(7) To use the technical term, he is the personal *perichoresis* of the Father in the Son, and of the Son in the Father.

Chapter Seven

The Lord and Giver of Life

In our final three chapters we turn from the noun in our title to the adjective. We have been thinking of the Spirit mainly as the Father's Gift to the Son and through the Son to us. This Gift is himself a person, a source and centre of initiatives and activities, and not a passive something to be possessed. As he is freely given by the Father, so also he freely gives; he is the Giving Gift. He is in Paul's words one who 'distributes his gifts to each exactly as he wills' (I Cor 12:11).

One of the limitations of the Augustinian understanding of the Spirit is its failure to do justice to the Spirit as active personal Giver. For many followers of Augustine to speak of the Holy Spirit and to speak of grace are just two ways of saying the same thing. Impersonal grace can very easily take the place of the personal Spirit, and be thought of as an inert thing that is passively handed over to us, so that it is at our disposal or even becomes part of ourselves.

In the New Testament and the Nicene creed the Holy Spirit is always 'the Lord' (II Cor 3:17), the free, personal, divine Giver who remains distinct from and unmastered by those to whom he gives himself and his gifts. The Spirit cannot be controlled or limited by any ecclesiastical system, by priestly power or by charismatic techniques, although all these manipulations have been attempted at different times in the history of the Church. He is as uncontrollable as the wind to which Jesus compared him in John 3:8; he gives what, when and to whom he himself wills.

What he gives is, according to the creed, life: he is 'the Lord and Giver of life.' The common element in all his diversity of gifts to us is that they are impartations of the divine life. If they do not manifest God's life in the community or the person to whom they are given, they cannot be the gifts of the Spirit of life. The Spirit gives us life, not as the source of it, which is the Father, not as the normative prototype of it, which is the risen Son, who is alive so fully and finally that he has done with death in all its forms for ever. The distinctive work of the Spirit is to communicate to us the life that is in the Father and the Son, so that we actually share and experience it in ourselves. In the Spirit the life that the Father wills and that the Son incarnates is brought over to our side of our relationship with them and begins to reach its destination in us as the first fruits of the whole human race for which it was intended.

The creed does not stop to explain what it means when it speaks of life in such close connection with the Holy Spirit. Is it the life that the Creator imparts to his whole animate creation and in a special way to humanity as represented by Adam in Genesis 2:7, 'The Lord God formed the man from the dust of the ground and breathed into his nostrils the breath (Hebrew *ruach* = spirit) of life and the man became a living being'? Or does it rather refer to the new life that Christ gives to his believing people and that they do not have apart from him and what he does for them? The creed does not tell us whether it is thinking of one of these or of both of them together, although the Old Testament orientation of what the Creed says about the work of the Spirit would point to the former rather than the latter.

In the New Testament the work of the Spirit is seen in the closest connection with the work of Christ and the new life that he brings, rather than in the context of creation. C.F.D. Moule puts it this way: 'In the New Testament . . . the Spirit is scarcely mentioned except as among Christians and as the agent of the "new creation", the bringing persons to "new life" in Christ . . . Christ as God's Wisdom and Word has cosmic functions, but not the Spirit.'[1] While, of course, it is taken for granted that the Spirit who came at Pentecost is the same Spirit who hovered creatively over the void and in whom Adam came to life, when the New Testament speaks of the Spirit it is not looking back to the origins of natural life, but forward to the life of the age to come which the Spirit makes present here and now through Christ. When the New Testament refers to creation it does so not in relation to the Spirit but in relation to the Son, the Word by whom all things were made (John 1:3).

For the New Testament the Spirit is not primarily the immanent presence of God in his creation; he is, rather, the mighty rushing wind and the consuming purifying fire that breaks in upon the creation to purify it from its past and to open it to its future. He is not the Spirit of things as they are, of the *status quo*, but rather the Spirit of the future, the Spirit of things as they are to be when the purpose of God for his creation is complete. It is no accident that on the day of Pentecost Peter turns to the book of Joel to find a key by which he can understand what is happening. '"In the last days," God says, "I will pour out my Spirit on all flesh"'(Acts 2:17 quoting Joel 2:28 ff). The exciting thing about Pentecost is not the tongues and prophecies or the signs and wonders. To be obsessed by the dramatic and sensational nature of the signs is to be in danger of forgetting what they are signs of. For Peter they are signalling that the last days have come, that the Spirit has begun his ultimate work in the regeneration, empowering and transformation of our human nature to make it ready for the appearing of the eschatological kingdom of God. The life of which the Spirit is Lord and Giver is *zoe aionia*, eternal life, or more accurately, the life of the age to come.

Because that is its perspective, the New Testament has little to say about the work of the Spirit in creation, and, if we were to examine the evidence, we would find that, apart from some eloquent hints, like those in Genesis we have already mentioned, the Old Testament has no clearly worked out teaching on this subject either. In fact, much Old Testament teaching about the Spirit, as for example the famous vision of the valley of dry bones in Ezekiel 37, is not so much about the power that indwells creation, but more about the power that rescues it from death and resurrects it into its new future with God.

That certainly does not mean that the Spirit is not centrally involved in the creative process. Father, Son and Holy Spirit are all involved in all the works of the one God, each in the way appropriate to him. The new creation (*kaine ktisis*) is the old creation radically renewed. The Spirit who is the agent of that renewal is the same Spirit who at the beginning brought order and vitality to the formless void and breathed into mankind the very life of God.

What, however, the New Testament approach is saying is that the work of the Spirit at the origin of things, like the work of the Spirit at the ultimate end of things, cannot be understood directly in and for itself but only in relation to Christ the incarnate Word who is the power and presence of God right in the midst of things. Because he is the Alpha and Omega, the beginning and the ending, what God has done at our origin and what God will do at our perfecting can be understood only in relation to what he is doing in him. He is the beginning from which the world comes and the ending to which the world goes. In Jesus he appears in the midst of human history and shows us his face. In him the eternal relationships between Father, Son and Spirit, which we were made to image and will image perfectly in the end, are made manifest among us.

Thus, when we know what the Spirit does in relation to Christ, we shall know what to look for in order to see what he is doing in creation, and we shall discern the firstfruits of the harvest that will be ready for reaping at the end, the first instalment of the inheritance into full possession of which he will bring us on the last day. To discern what the Spirit has been doing from the beginning of creation and what he will do when the Lord comes in glory, we have to look at what he does in Christ and in those who have begun to share the new life that comes from Christ. What is of God in ordinary life is revealed when we enter into that new life, which is both the rebirth and the fulfilment of what went before and the promise of what is still to come.

Thus it is in a New Testament Christ-centred context that we have to ask and answer the questions: What is this new life of which the Spirit is Lord and Giver and what can we learn from it about the work of the Spirit in all creation and in the coming kingdom? What sort of life does he bring? To such questions we can begin to answer as follows:

1. *The life that the Spirit gives is responsiveness.* To be alive is to be in active, purposeful interaction with other things or people in the environment around you. To be dead is to fail or to be unable to make that kind of response; it is to be acted on but never to act, to be passive object rather than initiating and responsive subject.

In animals, including man, the basic interaction with the environment is breathing: it is in the taking in and giving out of air that life is maintained. No breath, no life. Precisely that basic dynamic interchange involved in breathing is the central biblical analogy for the Holy Spirit. Both *ruach* and *pneuma* are the ordinary Hebrew and Greek words for breath. He is the Spirit of dynamic interaction, of mutual receiving and giving which is of the very stuff of life itself. In all genuine giving and receiving, especially genuinely personal giving and receiving among people, the Lord and Giver of life is at work. The kingdom of God to which he is leading us is that society in which personal and political relationships are characterised by the ability of its members to give to and receive from one another at every level of its life. Such a society will be eternally alive with the life of God himself, in which Father and Son give themselves eternally each to the other in the Holy Spirit.

At the centre, therefore, of that responsiveness which is the hallmark of life in the Spirit is God's responsiveness to us and our responsiveness to God in Christ. This is, in fact, the central theme of the Christian gospel. In Christ God gives himself to all humanity in the Spirit; in Christ, who is the representative of humanity, we give ourselves back to God in the same Spirit. He responds to our plight in his grace and we respond to his grace in our gratitude. In Christ God's grace and our gratitude are incarnate and perfected in a single human life, and they are so by the action of the Holy Spirit upon and within him. Christ, therefore, is our life; in him the receiving of grace and the giving of gratitude are there for us and promised to us. It is the business of the Holy Spirit to work in us what he has already worked in Christ, and to bring us into that responsiveness in which we are open to receive what God gives us in Christ and to give ourselves back to God as Christ gave himself.

For Paul in Romans 6, baptism into Christ marks a conversion of our responsiveness. Outside Christ we were dead to God and alive to sin, but now we are 'dead to sin but alive to God in Christ Jesus' (Rom 6:11). Outside Christ we are so implicated in the fallenness of things and people that we are not free to know, worship or serve God rightly. In Christ we have come alive where we were dead, because we have regained our ability to make a right response to God and have, at least in principle, lost our ability to respond to sin.

In consistency with this, Paul makes it clear in I Corinthians that the knowledge of God is not a natural possession of man but is possible only by a liberating act of the Spirit in the closest relationship to the work of Christ on the cross. The definitive saving act of God in Christ remains incomprehensible to both Jews and Greeks until the Spirit makes them free to understand and respond to it: 'No one comprehends the thoughts of God except the Spirit of God' (I Cor 2:11). To know God is a gift of the life-giving Spirit.

If it is only in the Spirit that we can know God, equally it is only in the Spirit that we can obey him. Paul himself confesses in Romans 7 that he knows only too well what it is like to know God's will and yet not to be free to do it. The result is a moral paralysis, a frustration that is a kind of death and that makes Paul cry out, 'What a wretched man I am, who will rescue me from this body of death?' (Rom 7:24). Here also it is the Spirit who gives the ability to respond in obedience. 'For the law of the Spirit of life [note the connection between *Spirit* and *life*] in Christ Jesus has set me free from the law of sin and death' (Rom 8:2). The man who is not in the Spirit is in the flesh which 'does not submit to God's law nor can it do so' (Rom 8:7). The power to obey God is not a natural freedom but has to be recreated in us by the Spirit who is the Spirit of Christ.

In Pauline theology, outside Christ there is deadness, unresponsiveness in our relationship to God, both as regards knowledge and obedience. This deadness is depicted in darkest hues in Ephesians, which, whether written by Paul or not, faithfully represents the Pauline tradition. He reminds his readers that before their conversion, in spite of all their pagan religion, they were from a Christian perspective 'without God in the world' (2:12). This did not mean that the God and Father of Jesus Christ did not then know and love them, but it did mean that they were incapable of knowing and loving him. They were in fact 'dead in trespasses and sins' (2:1); 'But, because of his great love for us God, who is rich in mercy, made us alive with Christ even when we were dead in transgressions – it is by grace you have been saved' (2:5). There has taken place in us a work of spiritual regeneration here understood as a resurrection, a being raised from the dead along with Christ, so that those who could not respond to God now can and do respond to him, and have come into a new dynamic relationship of giving and receiving with him.

So, in the Christian life we are brought into a wholly new order of responsiveness to God and this is the work of the Holy Spirit. In John 3:3-5 (one of the central New Testament statements on this subject) seeing the rule of God and entering by baptism into the community in which that rule is exercised is described as being born from above of water and the Spirit into a new awareness of and obedience to what God is doing in Christ. So also in John 1:12-13, without an explicit reference to the Spirit, the power to become a child of God is a result of new birth in which God himself is the sole progenitor and in which no human father can have any part.

This emphasis on the Spirit as the creator and Giver of our responsiveness to God in Christ is central to the New Testament understanding of the Spirit in contexts where the rebirth and resurrection metaphors are not used. We need only remind ourselves again that it is by the Spirit that we worship God as *Abba* (Gal 4:6) and confess Jesus as *Lord* (I Cor 12:3). Our responsiveness is not just knowledge and obedience, it is also worship and confession, and the freedom for both is the Spirit's gift to us.

It seems to me that in much contemporary Christianity the Spirit as the creator and Giver of our responsiveness is not properly recognised. On the more conservative side, in both its evangelical and catholic forms, there has been such a one-sided emphasis on the objective authority of the teaching of the Church or of the witness of Scripture that these can often be imposed upon people in an authoritarian way which does not leave room for their own response to the gospel. John Calvin knew well that for the truth of the gospel to come to us there was required not merely submission to some external authority but the *testimonium internum Sancti Spiritus*, the internal witness of the Holy Spirit, so that we could hear God speaking and come to affirm the truth of the gospel *for ourselves*, and not on the say-so of some ecclesiastical authority or holy book.[2]

On the other hand so much contemporary theology of a more liberal kind has escaped from such authoritarianism only to put its trust instead in the techniques of understanding and interpretation that comprise the new science of hermeneutics. As a result it can easily fail to notice that the very documents it is so concerned to interpret aright are quite clear that without the Holy Spirit we shall never know God or his truth. The techniques of biblical scholarship can certainly bring us to a more accurate appreciation of what the biblical writers are saying; but, to bring us to a conviction of the truth of the gospel and a relationship with the God of whom it speaks is the prerogative of the Holy Spirit alone.

Against the authoritarians we must assert the need to know the gospel *for ourselves*, and against those who put their trust in hermeneutical techniques, we must insist that we shall never know the gospel *by ourselves* and may be in danger of conforming its truth to techniques and presuppositions that are alien to that truth, rather than letting the truth transform our minds and our whole way of thinking about God and man.

In a similar way, we may fail to take seriously enough the New Testament requirement that we should respond for

ourselves to the gospel, by laying all the emphasis on Christ's
perfect response to God made on our behalf and in our place.
We have already identified such a tendency in the work of
T.F. Torrance. In Karl Barth also there is a strain of teaching
which comes near to suggesting that the work of the Spirit is
to convince us that Christ has vicariously responded to God
on our behalf, rather than bringing us to respond *for
ourselves* to what Christ has done.[3] It is indeed true that our
life is located in Christ, but it is the work of the Spirit to get us
into that life and that life into us, by enabling us to respond to
him for ourselves. Christ answers for us to God, but the Spirit
enables us to make our own what he has done by saying our
own Amen to it. Christ says 'Yes' to God for us, but the Spirit
liberates us to say 'Yes' to Christ for ourselves.

For ourselves, but not *by* ourselves. The 'pelagian' English,
to say nothing of the 'arminian' Americans, who seem
sometimes to believe in the power of human free will more
than they believe in the power of God, need constantly to be
reminded that it is not in the power of fallen humanity to say
'Yes' to what God has done for us in Christ. Left to ourselves
we are indeed dead in sins and trespasses. If we were free in
ourselves there would be no need of the liberating Spirit to
enable us to relate to *Abba* and *Kurios*. It is not that he
responds instead of us – that is what Christ does – but rather
that he enables us to do what we could not do without him
and respond for ourselves.

In other words he is the Lord and Giver of the new life of
responsiveness to God that Christ has won for us. He is its
Lord, because it belongs to him and not to us and comes to us
from him, but he is the Giver of it because it really does come
to us from him. The 'Yes' that we say to God in Christ is our
own 'Yes'; yet it is ours not as an achievement that has its
source in us, but as a gift of which the Giver is the Life-giving
Spirit. The paradox that we have summed up in the phrase
'*for* ourselves but not *by* ourselves' is the mystery of his
relationship with us.

In what the Spirit does in Christ and in us who believe in
Christ we have the clue to what he is doing in creation: he is
promoting responsiveness. If we were left to ourselves

outside Christ, then indeed we would be more and more unresponsive to God, to one another and to the world around us. We live in a society where the failure in responsiveness between individuals, between rich and poor, nation and nation, race and race is everywhere in evidence with devastating and often fatal consequences.

The human world has fallen into unresponsiveness; yet it is still the world God made, where his Spirit is at work. Wherever people give themselves to and for one another and relate with sensitivity to the created order, there are signs of the Spirit's activity, even where there is still no responsiveness to the good news of what God has done in Christ. Amidst the wages of sin that are death, there are still many signs of the presence and activity of the Lord and Giver of life.

Also, in what the Spirit does in Christ and in those who believe in Christ we have the clue to what he will finally do for all humanity. Our partial responsiveness to God in Christ is the first instalment (*arrabon* Eph 1:14), and firstfruits, (*aparche* Rom 8:23) of that complete responsiveness to God and his creation that is the future of all for whom Christ offered himself to the Father. In Jesus, the man in whom the Spirit abides in all his fullness and in the way he responds to his Father, to his people, to his world, we see the promise of what through the activity of the Spirit we shall all become.

To make us responsive with his responsiveness and alive with his life is the crowning work of the Spirit of life. He has begun to do that now and will not stop until the work is complete.

2. *The life the Spirit gives is purposefulness.* All living things are activated by purposes of which they are in different degrees aware, but which give shape and meaning to all that they do and are. They feed themselves, express themselves, defend themselves and reproduce themselves. To engage in these purposeful activities is to be alive. People without a purpose soon become bored and only half alive; those whose main purposes in life have all been frustrated do not long find life worth living. This is why poverty, unemployment, physical and mental disability are such threats to the quality of a person's or a society's life.

The Spirit of life is, therefore, the Spirit of purposefulness. If again we seek the clue to his activities in Christ and in those who believe in Christ, we shall see that his concern is to restore and fulfil us by enabling us to participate in God's great purpose which is to bring back humanity and the created order into right relationship to himself, so that they may share in his fullness of life. It is in these terms that Jesus defines his own central part in fulfilling his Father's purpose: 'I have come that they may have life and have it to the full' (John 10:10).

In the gospel we see God fulfilling that purpose not by the naked exercise of divine power but through his Son made man and anointed with the Holy Spirit. Jesus is the man on whom the Spirit in his baptism descends and rests. So it is a messianic work, the work of the prophet, priest and king who is endowed with the Spirit of God for the discerning and effecting of the divine purpose which the Father has committed to him.

The kingdom of God is inaugurated by the work of a Spirit-filled man and it is extended likewise by anointed men and women on whom the Spirit rests. The purpose of God is to be fulfilled through people, who have been set free from the small world of their own human purposes into an identification with their heavenly Father's purpose. Their motivating desire and prayer is that his kingdom should come and his will be done on earth as it is in heaven. They are equipped to do the work of God by the messianic Spirit that rested first on Jesus. To be called by Christ is to be called, like the first disciples, both into his company and into his service, to engagement with and involvement in the purpose that is his life (Mark 3:14). The service of the kingdom of God is varied enough to give purpose, and therefore life, to everyone whom Jesus calls.

In his baptism Jesus becomes the messianic Man who serves his Father by identifying himself with sinners, with the oppressed, the poor and the broken. So our baptism into him is our recruitment into the fulfilment of those purposes which he receives from his Father. His messianic mission continues and in it we are to find the purpose of our own lives. Our baptism is not only the sacrament of our regeneration, but, also, like the baptism of Jesus, is the sacrament of our commissioning into his messianic mission. Our primary temptation as Christians, like the temptations of the newly-baptised Jesus, is to withdraw from that mission into self-indulgence, self-assertion and compromise: our vocation, like that of Jesus, is to find our part in the work of God, as Luke 4:18 defines it. All the baptised are to say with him whose baptism they share, 'The Spirit of the Lord is upon me, because he has anointed me to bring good news to the poor. He has sent me to proclaim freedom for the prisoners and recovery of sight for the blind, to release the oppressed, to proclaim the year of the Lord's favour.'

These are things that we can only do if the 'Spirit of the Lord is upon us.' One of the great contributions of the charismatic renewal has been to remind us of that fact. Unfortunately, some of those who have claimed to be full of the Spirit and to be exercising his gifts have not always remembered that the purpose of that fullness and these gifts is to equip us for participation in God's mission of renewal to his creation.

The accounts that John and Luke give of the post-resurrection bestowal of the Spirit on the disciples differ as to date and context; but they are at one in emphasising that the Spirit is given to recruit and empower the disciples in their master's mission. In John 20 Jesus says, 'Receive the Holy Spirit' (v 22) to those to whom he has just said, 'As the Father sent me, I am sending you' (v 21). And in Acts 1:8 he says: 'You will receive power when the holy Spirit comes upon you, you will be my witnesses.' The Church's pentecostal baptism in the Spirit is its baptism into its part in the mission of its Lord to the ends of the earth and to the end of the age. According to Eduard Schweizer: 'The peculiarity of Luke's testimony lies in its demonstration that a church which has no special power to fulfil its missionary task in a concrete way is a church without the Spirit'.[4]

Thus the only convincing evidence that we have shared in the Church's baptism in the Spirit is not tongues, prophecies, healing, as such, but the use of these and countless other gifts

in a way that is effective in enabling people to see and enter
the kingdom of God. The test question for those who make
charismatic claims is not, 'How many gifts have you
exercised?', but, 'How many people and situations have you
brought into the kingdom and to the king?' Where gifts are
not exercised as tools for mission, they can easily become, as
Paul discovered at Corinth and many have discovered since,
tools of exhibitionism or the greedy search for self-fulfilment.

The Spirit communicates to us the messianic purposes of
God in Jesus and empowers us to take our part in fulfilling
them. He gets us moving in the same direction as Jesus in
trust and obedience to the same Father. He enables us to
share in Christ's love, in his authority and in his suffering. In
the Spirit we discover that when we subordinate and even
sacrifice our own purposes to those of God and when we
deny ourselves and take up our cross and follow, we do not
lose but gain; we do not narrow and circumscribe our lives
but rather expand and extend them, so that they come alive
with the life of God. The Lord and Giver of life takes us out of
ourselves and lets us find ourselves in a new way as we give
ourselves to his Father's mighty purposes.

If, therefore, the work of the Spirit in relation to Christ is
to integrate us into the purpose of God, his work before and
outside Christ can be recognised in all the purposes that men
and women undertake which reflect the priorities and values
of the kingdom, even when they have not yet acknowledged
the Lordship of the King. There are many human purposes
and enterprises that contradict and work against the
purposes of the kingdom, but there are some that at least
partially promote, proclaim, and anticipate that kingdom.
Where that is so, the life-giving Spirit is at work.

In the same way the *eschaton*, the ultimate end towards
which the Spirit works is the completion of that kingdom. It
is complete already in the risen Jesus who is the controlling
centre of the coming society of God's new people, and it
appears in part already in the Christian community. Its life is
life in the Spirit, when its purposes and priorities reflect those
of the Father who has revealed his kingdom in his Son.

3.   *As well as responsiveness and purposefulness, life is*

creativity. Inanimate things persist: living things grow, increase, achieve, procreate and multiply. In the Genesis story God's blessing upon the man and the woman made in his own image consists in his gift of his creativity and his command that they should use that gift. 'God blessed them and said to them, "Be fruitful and increase in number, fill the earth and subdue it. Rule... over every living creature that moves on the ground"' (Gen 1:28).

The human story on its positive side, sin apart, is the story of man's exercise of his God-given creativity, so as to advance from one degree of human glory to another. His achievements in actualising the potentialities of his environment and in subduing the earth to his purposes, not least in our own day, are awesome and vast. In his creaturely way he images the creativity of the God who made him and is meant so to do.

Yet, in all the forms that we know it, human creativity is marred by the fallenness of the people who exercise it. Human achievement and culture are highly ambiguous. We have only to look at the nuclear dilemma to see that the achievements of our creativity threaten to become the means of our ultimate destruction. Fallen Adam does not lose his creativity but begins to use it in ways that will bring about not the fulfilment but the destruction of his own life and that of his world. Precisely in regard to the results of our creativity, we need to be recreated. Our creativity needs to be brought back into relationship and constructive conformity to the creativity of God from which it sprung, but from which it has broken away.

Man, creatively transformed from the way God made him at the beginning into the way God wanted him at the end, has not yet appeared except definitively in the risen Christ and partially in those who belong to him. Jesus, the man who in his death and resurrection has borne and conquered sin, is in the empowering of the Spirit transformed into the *eschatos Adam*, the ultimate man, who has reached the *telos*, the end for which God made him. In his resurrection we see at work the recreating Spirit delivering the incarnate Son out of the limitations and frustrations of the old fallen creation into

that glorious liberty God has always intended for his people.
He is creatively transformed and transfigured into man as
he was always meant to be. According to I Corinthians
15:45, the ultimate man does not keep his transfigured life
to himself, but becomes life-giving Spirit, who conveys that
resurrecting transformation to his people. According to II
Corinthians 3:18 the work of the Spirit is to change and
transform us into the likeness of the risen Lord, so that the
glory of his love and power begin to appear in us.

The Spirit is the artist who shapes his people into countless
creative portrayals of the risen Lord. First, with Jesus he
changed the crucified humanity into the risen humanity in a
way that preserved its identity but brought it to its fulfilment.
Then, secondly in us, he takes the human material that
makes you you and me me and, in a way that is authentic
to what God made us and that preserves our created identity, he sets us free from our fallenness and begins to sanctify
and transform us into yet another portrait of Christ.

He is the saint-making Spirit. Saints are on the one hand
true to themselves, their times and their culture. They are
inexplicable except in terms of the blood they inherit and
the soil from which they spring.

Out of that material, respecting all that is of God in it,
the creator Spirit brings forth a new likeness of Jesus. There
are no stereotypes of sanctity. All the saints are gloriously
various, but out of all the differing colours and textures of
their created natures and personalities the Spirit sets himself
to paint a new ikon of the Lord. Being thus in process of
being recreated by the Spirit, saints begin to be themselves
recreative in the communities and societies to which they
belong.

When we see humanity transfigured by the Spirit, fully in
Christ and partially in his saints, we have the clue by which
we can discern and trace the creative activity of the Spirit
before and outside Christ, and by which we can look forward
towards the end, when that Christ-shaped transfiguration
will have been completed in the whole new creation. The
Lord and Giver of Life brings the incarnate Son to birth in
full responsiveness to God and man. He baptises and

empowers him at Jordan into God's great purpose for him. He recreates him in his resurrection into the final glory of his humanity. When we see the fullness of life he gives to the Son, we see also the fullness of life that he promises and has begun to give to us. From that perspective we see how he begins his work in the fallen creation and how he will complete it in the coming kingdom of God. In the life he gives to the Son, we see him as the Giver of all life, and we are opened up to the promise of the responsive, purposeful, creative life that he has started to bring from Christ to us.

Notes on Chapter Seven

(1) C.F.D. Moule, *The Holy Spirit*, London, Mowbrays, 1978, pp 19–20.
(2) John Calvin, *Institutes of the Christian Religion*, John T. McNeill ed., Philadelphia, Westminster Press, 1960, Vol 1, pp 78–81.
(3) See especially his teaching about faith as acknowledgment, recognition and confession in *Church Dogmatics*, IV:1., ET Edinburgh, T. & T. Clark, 1956, pp 757ff.
(4) E. Schweizer 'Spirit of God' in Kittel's *Theological Dictionary of the New Testament*, London, ET, Adam and Charles Black, 1960, p 50.

Chapter Eight

The Giver of Fellowship

If the central thesis of this book is correct, it is not surprising that Paul should describe the Spirit as the creator of *koinonia*, fellowship, in II Corinthians 13:14. As the Son is characterised by the grace he embodies and as the Father is characterised by the love of which he is the source, so the Spirit is characterised by the *koinonia* in which his own person is rooted and which he produces in us as the primary result of his presence and activity among us.

The word *koinonia*, in the Greek of the New Testament, has a strong meaning which is inadequately represented by the English word, fellowship, which, especially in a religious context, is often weak and vague in meaning. The root meaning of *koinonia* is a having in common, the sharing of a common life. It can be used to describe an intimate spiritual union of persons, but words from the same root can equally well be used to describe the sharing of money and possessions, which was one of the first results of the pouring out of the Spirit at Pentecost. 'All the believers were together and had everything in common (*hapanta koina*)' (Acts 2:44).

According to I John 1:3 the creation of this *koinonia* is the primary purpose and effect of the proclamation of the gospel: 'We proclaim to you what we have seen and heard, so that you also may have *koinonia* with us. And our *koinonia* is with the Father and with his Son Jesus Christ'. These two occurrences of the word clearly indicate the two dimensions of the *koinonia* which the gospel creates. On the hand it is a *horizontal* sharing of life among believers: on the other it is a *vertical* sharing of life between believers on the one side and the Father and the Son on the other. One could hardly think of a more theologically succinct and practically challenging description of the Church. The Christian Church is, in the purpose and intention of God, that community of people who, as a result of their hearing and believing of the gospel, have been enabled to share through Christ in God's own life, and who, as a result, have begun to share their lives with one another on every level. It is a norm that very few congregations live up to; yet the more they are in Christ and the more the Spirit sets them free, the nearer they come to it.

In the rest of his first letter one of John's central themes is that vertical *koinonia* with God and horizontal *koinonia* with one another are so inseparably connected that you cannot have the one without the other. The only way that one can have *agape*-love for God's people is by being 'born of God', and, on the other hand, to fail to love your brother on the visible level is a sure sign that you do not love God on the invisible level. 'Every one who loves has been born of God and knows God. Whoever does not love does not know God, because God is love' (4:7-8). 'If anyone says, "I love God", yet hates his brother, he is a liar. For anyone who does not love his brother whom he has seen, cannot love God whom he has not seen' (4:20).

The inseparability of our new relationship with God in Christ and our resultant and very practical sharing of life with one another is demonstrated in Acts 2, precisely in the context of the coming of the Spirit at Pentecost. His coming results, first of all, in the apostles sharing in the authority and power of the risen and exalted Jesus. The preached word of Peter has converting effect on a large scale and the prayer of Peter and John over the lame man at the gate of the temple in the next chapter (Acts 3:6-10) results in his miraculous healing. No sooner is their new sharing through the Spirit in the power of Jesus inaugurated than it results, as we have already indicated, in a new sharing among themselves in spiritual, social and economic ways, 'All the believers were together and had everything in common. Selling their possessions and goods, they gave to anyone as he had need.

Every day they continued to meet together in the temple courts. They broke bread in their homes and ate together with glad and sincere hearts' (2:44–46). The key word in that passage is undoubtedly 'together'. The sharing of one Spirit results in their co-ordination into one body in all sorts of visible and practical ways.

One of my very few criticisms of Richard Lovelace's fine book, *Dynamics of Spiritual Life,* concerns the way in which he relegates what he calls the 'community of believers' to the 'secondary elements' of renewal.[1] Such teaching seems to me to owe more to Protestant individualism than to the New Testament. In the gospel, being in Christ and being in the closest fellowship with other Christians are too inseparably connected for one to be thought of as secondary to the other. To be in Christ and to be in the Church, *i.e.* the visible company of believers, are one and the same thing. If you are not in Christ, you are not in the Church: if you are not in the Church, you are not in Christ. To be baptised into Christ is to join a local visible community which is the body of Christ in that place. Any baptism that does not entail the integration of the baptised into the local community of believers in which that baptism is performed is so far a defective baptism. Belonging to the Church is not a secondary consequence of our relationship to Christ but an essential and defining component within it.

The Holy Spirit is the Spirit of relationship: as he opens us up to the Father and the Son, he opens us up to one another as well. Where we stand with the Holy Spirit is much more clearly demonstrated by the state of our relationships with other people than it is by the dramatic gifts that we exercise. The *charismata* are secondary to the *koinonia*. The initial evidence that we share in the Church's baptism in the Spirit is less speaking in tongues and more new relationships of love with God and with others.

The Church, Body of Christ and Temple of
the Holy Spirit

So, to put the matter in more Pauline terminology, to be in the one Spirit involves incorporation into the one body over which Christ is the one head. Our purpose in this chapter is to ask how we are to understand the Church as both the body of Christ and the temple of the Holy Spirit. The life of God's people has both a christological and a pneumatological dimension. The main traditions in western Christianity have tended to understand the Church in its relation to Christ as his body, but revival movements of all kinds, of which Pentecostalism is a typical modern representative, have tended to see the Church as the fellowship in which the Spirit works and dwells. We need to ask how the minority tradition of understanding the Church in terms of the Spirit relates to the majority tradition of understanding it in terms of Christ. Our whole approach in this book to the Christ-Spirit relation will predispose us to think that the two traditions are complementary rather than contradictory; it is a case of both-and rather than of either-or.

Christ is the king and head of the Church. As such he stands over against it as the one from whom it has its origin, who is the norm to which all its life is to be conformed, and into whose likeness and completeness it has more and more to grow. We are in the Church when we stand in that sort of relationship to Christ, when we confess *Iesous Kurios,* Jesus is Lord.

Christ is not only transcendent to the Church as its king and head. By the Holy Spirit he is made present and powerful not just outside us and apart from us at the right hand of the Father, but on our side of the relationship, in us and among us. His life, his love, his power, he himself is in the Holy Spirit immanently at work among us. The Spirit establishes him in life-sharing *koinonia* with us, and us in life-sharing *koinonia* with him. In other words, we are the Church because we are related in him; it is the Spirit who does the relating and who ensures that it is the uniquely intimate kind of relating portrayed in the New Testament.

This *koinonia* is nothing less than the participation of human persons in the life of the incarnate Son in such a way that everything is shared between them. At the same time he remains who he is in his personal distinctness from them and equally they remain who they are in their distinctness from him. Through the Holy Spirit we respond to the person of Christ in our own persons and so become his body, the earthly expression of his now ascended divine and human life. All this is impossible apart from the work of the Holy Spirit, who in the incarnation has taken all that is ours and made it his, and who now takes all that is his and makes its ours (cf John 16:14-15).

In Roman Catholicism the Church has often been described as the extension of the incarnation. It is a description liable to more than one serious objection, not least from our point of view because it defines the Church exclusively in terms of Christ and says nothing about its relation to the Spirit. Against this Heribert Mühlen proposes that the Church should be understood rather as the extension of the baptism of Jesus.[2] The Church's relationship to Christ, he argues, is quite different from the relationship of Godhead and manhood in the incarnation. There God and man are united in the single person of the incarnate Son. In himself the Son is a single person who is both God and man and not a relationship between two persons.

The Church cannot rightly be described as the extension of the incarnation because its relationship to Christ is not like that. However close the union between Christ and his people, it remains a relationship of persons who have to retain their personal distinctness over against one another precisely in order to be able to relate to one another. A personal relationship by definition requires two distinct parties who give it its special quality by their free decision to enter into it. The assumption of humanity by the Son of God, which is what we mean by the incarnation, lacks that dimension of personal relationship between two persons, and therefore it is not a good model for understanding how the Church is related to Christ.

In the baptism of Jesus on the other hand, what happens is the intimate uniting of three distinct persons whose personal identity and integrity over against each other is maintained. The person of the Father gives himself to the person of the Son in the person of the Spirit in such a way that the personal distinctions between all three remain. The Father does not become the Son, nor does the Holy Spirit become the Son. The Father gives himself to his Son in the power of the Spirit, who is truly who he is within that act of self-giving. The Spirit is the Gift of the Father to the Son: he comes from the Father to the Son's side of the relationship. As the person who is given he remains distinct from the Son, the person to whom he is given. As the Giving Gift he transmits the life, love and power of the Father to the Son.

The unity of Son and Spirit involved in the baptism of Jesus does not abolish their identity as distinct persons. Mühlen calls it a personological unity, and holds that it is a good model of the sort of unity that the Spirit effects between Father, Son and believers in the Church. The union of Christ with the Church is also a personological unity *between* persons. That is why Mühlen proposes to describe the Christian community as the extension of the baptism of Jesus. In both the Spirit as distinct person unites other persons in such a way that they remain personally distinct from one another. The Son of God is not incarnate in the Church as he is incarnate in Christ: as one person he lives among and within many other persons in the power of the Spirit.

This is precisely the sort of union between Christ and his people that Paul describes in Ephesians 5:22-23, when he compares it to the union of husband and wife in marriage. 'The two become one flesh' (vv 31-32) without forfeiting their identity as two distinct persons. It is a unity of love, and because it takes two to love, the twoness is as integral to it as the oneness. The mystery of the Church is not that we are merged into Christ, still less that he is merged into us, but rather that he gives himself to us and we give ourselves to him. It is in the Spirit that this unity of life-sharing love between him and us is effected, because the Holy Spirit in all his activity in the life of God and in the life of man unites persons without merging them.

He is, in another of Mühlen's phrases, the one person in the many persons who makes them one without their ceasing to be themselves. The Spirit who joins us in one body to Christ himself remains a free person over against us, as we remain free persons over against him, exercising the liberty which is his gift to us (II Cor 3:17). In this unity the diversity of persons, far from being abolished, is rather affirmed and valued. In I Corinthians 12 the diversity of gifts and of the members of the body who exercise them is as important as the unity of the body to which they all belong. The one Spirit holds together the many members in such a way that the unity of the body is enriched by the diversity of the members and their gifts. 'We were all baptised by one Spirit into one body' is the basis of our unity; however, 'the body is not made up of one part but of many... If they were all one part, where would the body be? As it is there are many parts but one body' (vv 13,14,19,20). Here, equally emphasised, is the value of our diversity.

Of course, in this body all the parts are persons, so that it is a body of diverse persons with diverse functions and characteristics whose unity consists in the fact that the Holy Spirit has enabled them all to confess that Jesus is Lord and to be joined to him in the sharing of his life, love and power. The unity of the Church cannot be imposed by ecclesiastical authority from above, just as it cannot be created by democratic decision from below. It is not effected either by doctrinal consensus or the continuity of episcopal ministry in the Church. The principle of our unity, the one who gives and maintains it is the Holy Spirit. As we are open to him, so we shall find one another. One of the great enduring blessings of the charismatic renewal is that people who were deeply divided in doctrinal convictions and denominational loyalties have found, understood, learned from and started to love one another, because of what the Spirit has been doing in them all.

The Spirit, therefore, is not only the personal bond of unity within the life of God, proceeding from the Father to the Son to bind them together in their mutual self-giving: he is also the personal bond of unity of the Church who integrates people into the one life of Christ and so into one life with one another. The Church is not just a conglomerate of individual believers, or the sum of their relationships to God and one another. The Church has been anointed and baptised in the Holy Spirit since the day of Pentecost, and all her members have been baptised into her baptism and anointed with her anointing, even though they are not all equally or fully aware of it.

The Spirit at the Heart of the Church

In other words, the Spirit who comes from the Father through the Son is himself the mystery at the heart of the Church. He is the *paraklétos*, the one who comes to stand beside and among us on our side of our relationship with Christ, so that we can receive all that Christ has for us and give him all that he requires of us. He is in his person our *koinonia* with the Father and the Son and as such he is also the *koinonia* of all Christians with one another. If the Holy Spirit sometimes has to break *koinonia* for the sake of the truth of Christ, he will always be eager to re-establish it for the sake of the love of Christ.

The Holy Spirit is in the Church as the Lord and Giver of its new life in Christ. He is the gracious Giver of all renewed responsiveness, purposefulness and creativity among the people of God. The history of the Church is the record of his refusal to abandon people who have often done all they could to quench and grieve him. He is to be praised both for his glorious renewings and his unwavering faithfulness to his people in the long troughs of dullness and despondency.

The revivalist picture of the Spirit as a merely occasional visitor to the Church in its days of renewal with long periods of absence in between is nothing more than a parody and a travesty of Church history. Sometimes indeed the rivers of living water run underground for long stretches; yet even in the days of the Church's winter there are enough trees fruiting and flowering to show that the supernatural supplies are still being provided. When springtime at length returns, it is always the result of what the Spirit was doing in the winter that preceded it, when the Church seemed more than half dead.

The medieval Church on the eve of the Reformation, for example, was not plunged in the unrelieved blackness that Protestant polemics have sometimes suggested. As well as corrupt popes and venal pardoners, there were many who were praying for a new and better day, who were fed with the word amidst many errors and nourished with Christ's body and blood despite an erroneous sacramental theology. The seeds of the new summer were being sown and watered by the Spirit in the midst of the winter of the Church's discontent.

There is no resurrection without first there being a crucifixion, in which the last word seems to be with sin and deadness. For the eye of faith the Spirit who is openly at work in the resurrection is just as much secretly at work at the cross. He creatively reproduces in new contexts and fresh situations the pattern of God's work that is savingly and definitively revealed in God's incarnate Son. It is, therefore, always a way of dying and of coming to life. In the death there is promise of life, and in the life, until the ultimate resurrection, there is always the threat of death.

Movements of renewal and revival have in them not only the supernatural activity of the Spirit but also the upsurging of human exclusiveness, arrogance, disregard for truth and hunger for power that can frustrate and even threaten to neutralise what the Spirit is doing. The Church is never so dead as to have no promise and foretaste of new life within it: the Church is never so alive as to have no danger of decline and dissolution. What was true of the Corinthian charismatics has also been true of all their successors down the centuries. Amidst much that speaks of the Spirit there is mixed much that speaks of human immaturity and sinfulness.

In good days and bad, in high days and low, the Spirit continues his converting and sanctifying work among God's people. If he departed, the Church would cease. He may be grieved yet his grace persists; his fire may burn low yet cannot finally be quenched. He is the Spirit of him who raised up Christ from the dead and, therefore, he keeps on giving resurrection life to the body of Christ (Rom 8:11). As with the believer, so with the Church, the last enemy to be destroyed will be death (I Cor 15:26), and the ultimate future belongs to that life of which the Spirit here and now gives us the firstfruits and the promise.

Christ Institutes: the Spirit Constitutes

Thus, while the Church is totally dependent on the Spirit, in no sense is the Spirit dependent upon or at the disposal of the Church, so as to be at the beck and call of its sacramental ministers, ecclesiastical forms or charismatic techniques. As Yves Congar puts it: 'Ecclesiology is a function of pneumatology. In modern theology on the other hand one often gets the impression that pneumatology has become a function of ecclesiology, the Spirit has become a guarantor of the Church as institution.'[3]

The Spirit, in other words, does not guarantee and maintain an institutional life that the Church claims to have received from Christ by historical continuity or in some other way. It is by the action of the Spirit and not by any institutional means apart from the Spirit that the Church is related to Christ and receives his life. God's people have to seek the Spirit again and again both in order to have their confession, their worship, their mission and their fellowship reorientated to Christ and to be rescued from the damage done by human flesh which works destruction equally in the form of complacent frozen institutionalism and in the form of unbridled self-indulgent spontaneity. Regrettably, Catholics, Protestants, Pietists, and Charismatics all have their own typical ways of grieving the Spirit.

Professor John D. Zizioulas in his seminal book, *Being as Communion* (which is required, if demanding, reading for all who are interested in the Church's dependence on the Holy

Spirit), makes one of his major points as follows: 'Christ *in*-stitutes and the Spirit *con*-stitutes. The difference between these two prefixes 'in' and 'con' can be enormous ecclesiologically. The "institution" is something presented to us as a fact, more or less a *fait-accompli*. As such, it is a provocation to our freedom. The "constitution" is something that involves us in its very being, something we accept freely, because we take part in its very emergence. Authority in the first place is something imposed upon us, whereas in the latter it is something that springs from amongst us'.[4]

To understand Zizioulas' main point here, we need to forget the ordinary meanings of the words 'institution' and 'constitution' and concentrate on the prefixes 'in' and 'con'. By saying that the Church is *in*stituted by Christ he means that it is a community that is there before us. What the Church confesses in her worship, the life she lives in the world, the mission she undertakes to all peoples, are historically and normatively set by the incarnate Son – his teaching and still more his death and resurrection. We were not consulted about any of them and are not free to alter them. If we want to be identified with this institution, there are some things that we have simply to accept as having been laid down and given in the saving action of Christ, the Church's king and head.

We may argue, and frequently do, about precisely *what* Christ did lay down as necessary if the Church is to remain the Church that he founded. Does it, for example, include a form of Church government like the threefold ministry of bishops, priests and deacons? Most Christians would agree that, in principle, there is a central core of Christian belief and practice that has its origin and authority in Christ himself, what he said, did and was. If it denies or changes this core, the Church puts its very being as the body of Christ into jeopardy. The Church is from Christ and for Christ and will in the end be judged by Christ. This is what Zizioulas means when he says that the Church is *instituted* by Christ.

However, if we over-emphasise the given, 'institutional' element in the Church, as we often have in the West, we are in danger of imposing the gospel on people in a heteronomous and authoritarian way. Therefore, argues Zizioulas, it is important to take into account that the Church is not only *in*-stituted by the incarnate Son, but is *con*-stituted by the Holy Spirit. *Con* means together and, as we have been saying throughout this chapter, the Holy Spirit is the Spirit of *koinonia*, togetherness. The Spirit creates a togetherness between Christ and his people. For Christ is no longer simply the exalted king and head who imposes his 'institution' upon us. He is one with whom in the Spirit we have entered into such close person-to-person relationship, that his originally external authority over us is internalised, so that we, together with him, are saying our own free 'Yes' to what he has laid down for us.

In the Spirit we do not just submit to the gospel as something imposed upon us by Christ. We respond to it, as Peter did at Caesarea Philippi, freely and spontaneously *for* ourselves, although not *by* ourselves, because that freedom is itself the work and gift of the Holy Spirit. We do not simply repeat the Scriptures or the creeds: the Holy Spirit in the Church is the Spirit not of repetition but of creativity. The mark of his creativity is that the new response which he enables to arise in terms, say, of doctrinal and liturgical formulation, as well as new forms of witness or community life, is both faithful to what Christ has instituted, and also relevant to the people who make the response and to the historical and cultural situation in which it is made. Our response to the gospel needs to be both true to what Christ has given, and anchored in the time in which we live.

By his very nature the Holy Spirit will ensure that in our response we are both *faithful* and *relevant*. He comes from Christ and is one in being with Christ, so that he cannot in any way deny or contradict Christ. He comes to us on our side of our relationship with Christ to convert and liberate us, so that we can confess and serve Christ in a way that is authentic to ourselves and our time. To be faithful at the expense of relevance, like some conservative Christians, or to be relevant at the expense of faithfulness, like some radical Christians, is to fail in different ways to be open to the Spirit. He takes what is Christ's (all of it without dilution or

diminution) and makes it ours (really and authentically
ours). This is not achieved without strain and conflict, as we
know very well in our own day. Yet, if we are open to the
creativity of the Spirit, the Church will discover how both to
be faithful to be Christ's institution and to make a response to
the gospel that is contemporary and relevant to the society in
which we live.

We can explore and amplify this general point in a specific
way with reference to the central act of the Church's worship,
the eucharist. It is of the essence of the sacrament that it was
instituted by Christ. Its origin, its form and its content refer
to what he did at the meal in the upper room with his disciples
on the night that he was betrayed. In it we obey his specific
command, *Touto poieite eis ten emen anamnesin*, Do this in
remembrance of me (I Cor 11:24). In this sacrament there is
not only the observance of something that was historically
given by Jesus: there is also a togetherness, a *koinonia*, a real
presence of the risen and ascended Christ with his people,
which has its scriptural witness in the Emmaus story in Luke
24. He imparts himself to us as the bread of life that we are to
eat and so partake of, and share in, his eternal life (John 6:
48-51).

In modern western, as in classical eastern liturgy, the
enactment of this togetherness which makes the historical
Lord's Supper into the contemporary Holy Communion is
explicitly attributed to the Holy Spirit. Nearly all these
liturgies now have in their great eucharistic prayers what is
technically called an *Epiclesis*, a prayer invoking the Holy
Spirit to come either upon the bread and wine, or upon those
who will consume them, (and often upon both) to use the
given ritual of the sacrament to effect our *koinonia* with
Christ and with one another.[5]

To pray thus is to recognise that togetherness with Christ
cannot be brought about by the repetition of the words of
Jesus by an ordained minister in an approved historical
succession, nor by the remembering of him by the
communicants as a person in past history. It is the work of
the Holy Spirit, not of the priest or the congregation and
certainly not of the words of institution in and by themselves,

to bridge the distance of the centuries between us and the historical Jesus and the eschatological distance between us and the ascended Lord. He alone can bring us to him and him to us, so that we may share in his life and blessings.

So the eucharist, like the Church in which it is celebrated, is *instituted* by Jesus. Without that historical givenness it loses its content and its meaning. It is *constituted,* however, by the Holy Spirit. Without him it lacks, so to speak, its *con* factor, the togetherness of head and body, and remains simply commanded ordinance. The Spirit takes what Christ instituted and involves us in it, so that he is present with us to give and to receive and we are present with him to receive and to give.

What is true of the Church's central act of worship is also true of her whole life. The Church's preaching is, on the one hand, the exposition of the given word of Scripture, which it takes historical research and knowledge to understand. When we preach we are to say again what the Bible says and not something novel of our own. On the other hand, it is the Spirit working in the preacher and his hearers who alone can use that word to bring about a living encounter between us and the God who spoke first in Israel and then definitively in Christ and who speaks still. Likewise, it is the Spirit who works in preacher and congregation to ensure that what is said is not only faithful exposition of the words of Scripture but the application of these words in a way that makes them relevant to contemporary situations that are far beyond the contemplation or understanding of the scriptural authors, so that contemporary people can make a contemporary response.

So also in the organisation of the Church there are given institutions like Bible, sacrament, and, many would say, ministry, which are in historical continuity with the work of Jesus, pointing us to him as source and norm. There is also the Spirit who makes word and sacrament the means of our *koinonia* with Christ and gives to the ministries that he instituted charismatic gifts of word and action, like prophecy and healing, by which we come into dynamic participation in Christ's risen life and power.

That charismatic element is truly Christian only when it remains in conformity with what is given in Christ. Prophets and charismatics of all kinds are to be recognised as being of God only if they confess that Jesus Christ has come in the flesh (I John 4:1-3). Faithfulness to the once given gospel is the first mark of charismatic authenticity. Between him and his ministers there is not only an external correspondence and a historical connection. By the Spirit they are enabled to share in his mind, his love, his power and his life in a way that is constantly fresh, spontaneous and creative. Jesus instituted the apostolate as the organisational structure of the new Israel. From that institution the Church's ministries are historically derived. And these ministries are constituted in contemporary dynamic and relevant effectiveness by the charismatic action of the Holy Spirit. In the Church and its members there are both faithful memories of Jesus and contemporary manifestations of his living presence and power.

So, to sum up, if the Church does not relate itself to its institution by Christ, it can easily become an autonomous religious fellowship, with no norms but its own experience, with ultimate authority located in itself, claiming to discern the speaking and action of God in all sorts of other places beside the Word that became incarnate in Jesus. When spiritual freedom and creativity are prized and promoted in and for themselves without responsibility towards what is given in the gospel, the spirit at work in that Church is not the Spirit of Jesus. At best it is the spirit of a God who can be known and met apart from Jesus, and at worst the spirit of the Church itself and of the age to which it belongs. Further if the Church forgets that it is the Spirit who again and again constitutes it in vitality and creativity, it can easily become formal and fossilised, confessing as the sole norm of its life the external authority of Christ and his gospel expressed either in the apostolic ministry or the apostolic Scriptures or in some combination of both. It can be solidly orthodox and virtually spiritually dead, robbed of its spontaneity and unable to bring together the Christ to whom it witnesses and the world in which it lives.

By institution the Church is the body of Christ and by constitution it is the *koinonia* of the Holy Spirit, the company of those who have been made free by the Spirit to receive and to give themselves to what the Father gives them in the Son, and out of that relationship to him to be drawn into the sort of togetherness with one another which enables them credibly to proclaim the Father through the Son and in the power of the Spirit to the world.

In the day-to-day life of the Church there is often tension between being faithful to what Christ has given and being relevant to the world in which we live. It is all too possible for this tension to be resolved in ways that are fatal to the gospel and its communication. Nevertheless, there is a creative way of living with tension that refuses either to accommodate what Christ has given to the prevailing culture, or to withdraw from that culture behind the high walls of a Christian ghetto, and in one way or the other to grieve the Spirit. He is *both* the Spirit of Christ who makes us faithful to Christ *and* he is the Spirit who comes to our side of the relationship with Christ to set us free to respond to Christ in a manner that is authentic to our time and place in God's world and which, therefore, the contemporary world can understand.

To explore fully this approach to an understanding of the Church, taking equally seriously both the christological and pneumatological dimensions of its life and exploring in detail the relationship between them, is far beyond the scope of this chapter. Here we could only attempt the barest outlines of an ecclesiology which takes seriously the distinctive work of the Holy Spirit, who alone can effect the togetherness of the people of God in one shared life with one another and with the Father and the Son.

Notes on Chapter Eight

(1)   Richard Lovelace, *Dynamics of Spiritual Life,* Exeter, Paternoster, 1979, pp 16ff.

(2) Heribert Mühlen, *Una Mystica Persona,* 1964, Ch 7. para 60.
(3) Yves Congar, *I Believe in the Holy Spirit,* Vol II, ET, London, Geoffrey Chapman, 1983, p 46.
(4) John D. Zizioulas, *Being as Communion,* London, Darton, Longman and Todd, 1985, p 140.
(5) The so-called Lima document, *Baptism, Eucharist and Ministry,* (Geneva, World Council of Churches 1982, p 13 paras 15 and 16 and Commentary) insists that bread and wine become the sacramental signs of Christ's body and blood in virtue of *both* the word of Christ (institution) *and* the power of the Holy Spirit (constitution). It sees in this recognition the possibility of a new ecumenical solution to some hitherto intractable problems in sacramental theology.

Chapter Nine

The Giver of Worship

The Christian community's dynamic sharing of life with God is its worship. The love with which he has given himself to us in Christ draws from us an answering love in which we give ourselves to him. We give ourselves in direct response to God's love in praise. We give ourselves for the sake of others in intercession. We give ourselves by seeking for ourselves the closer relationship with him that comes when we confess our sins or open our needs to him. In answering these different kinds of prayer, God responds to our response to him by giving himself afresh to us.

The Holy Spirit, who is the Spirit of divine self-giving, is intimately involved in the prayer and worship of the Church, precisely because prayer and worship have to do with dynamic mutual self-giving within the relationship that God in Christ has established with his people. In this final chapter we shall be trying to understand more precisely how the Spirit operates in the life-exchanging intimacies of that relationship.

We shall be able to see better how the Spirit is at work in the life of prayer if we remind ourselves briefly of how he operates within the trinitarian life of God himself. The Spirit, as we have seen, has the source of his being in the Father's Gift of himself to the Son, and he is the personal expression of the Son's responsive self-giving to the Father. Just as a child expresses in a third person the love of his parents, so the Spirit expresses in his person the initiating love of the Father for the Son and the responsive love of the Son for the Father.

The mutual self-giving of Father and Son in the Spirit is of the very essence of the life of God.

That self-giving is both creative and redemptive, so that our creation and our redemption have their source in it. We were made by a God who is self-giving in himself, in order that he might give himself to us and that we might give ourselves to him and to one another. We are redeemed because on the cross the Son gave himself to the Father in intercession for us, and because the Father in response to that intercession gave his life afresh to his incarnate Son by raising him from the dead.

When the Son of God becomes incarnate as man in Jesus Christ, the eternal divine interchange of mutual self-giving in the Spirit takes the form of human prayer. This man who kneels in the early morning on a Galilean hillside or late at night in a Jerusalem garden called Gethsemane is the eternal Son receiving from and giving himself to his Father. In fact, if prayer is at its heart creative and redemptive self-giving, then the whole life of Jesus is prayer, in which in trust and obedience he offers himself for us to the Father. This is why he can teach with authority and heal with power. His self-giving reaches its climax on the cross, which itself can be most helpfully understood as intercession – the self-offering of the eternal Son to the eternal Father on behalf of mankind from the midst of the extremities of human sin and suffering.[1]

Where there is this kind of self-giving, there also is the Holy Spirit. It is significant that Luke, who is particularly interested in the prayer life of Jesus, should make one of his rare mentions of the Holy Spirit in the post-baptism ministry in connection with one of the high points in Jesus' prayer relationship to the Father. 'At that time Jesus, full of joy through the Holy Spirit, said, "I praise you, Father, Lord of heaven and earth, because you have hidden these things from the wise and learned and revealed them to little children"' (Luke 10:21). He prays rejoicingly to the Father in the Holy Spirit. It is the Spirit who joins Father and Son in such a close relationship that no one can know the one apart from the action of the other (v 22). Here it becomes for once explicit that Jesus' relation with *Abba*, which is central both to his

praying and to everything else that he does, is a relationship
in the Holy Spirit.

If the prayer of Jesus is 'in the Spirit', so also is ours
according to Ephesians 6:18: 'Pray in the Spirit on all
occasions with all kinds of prayers and requests.' Notice 'all
kinds of prayers' are to be prayed in the Spirit. Prayer in the
Spirit is not one special kind of prayer, like, for example,
praying in tongues. Just as there can be no authentically
Christian prayer apart from the mediation of the Son, so
equally there can be no effective Christian prayer apart from
the activity of the Holy Spirit. To put the same point
positively, all Christian prayer and worship are the gift of the
Holy Spirit. We are much more inclined to regard prayer as
duty demanded from us rather than as gracious gift offered to
us – something that we have to do for God, rather than
something that God does in us.[2] It is helpful to look more
closely at what is involved in these two contrasting
approaches to worship, and to ask ourselves as we do this,
which one better describes the basic attitude with which we
ourselves come to the worship of the Church and to our own
prayers.

Prayer as Task

According to the first approach, prayer is primarily a task for
us to fulfil, something that we have to do at the right time, in
the right way, in order, if not to establish, at any rate to
maintain our relationship with God. He has come and
liberated us for himself in Christ: our responsibility in prayer
is to keep coming to him. If we do, the relationship will
prosper and deepen; if we do not, it will loosen and weaken.
The onus is on us.

On such a view the central place of the Spirit in the life of
worship will almost inevitably be neglected and misunderstood. He may be seen as God's answer to our prayer, but
hardly as the gracious promoter of our praying. For, on this
model, God is not at our end of the prayer relationship. He is
separate from us and has to be reached by us. Our prayer is

aimed at him as its target, like an arrow shot from a bow. If we do not aim the arrow in the right direction or if there is not enough tension in the bowstring, the arrow may not reach the centre of the target. If we do not pray for the right thing in the right way and if we do not pray often enough or believingly enough, our prayer will not reach God and therefore will not be answered.

To view prayer in this manner almost inevitably promotes crippling anxiety when we do pray and paralysing guilt when we fail to pray. 'Am I doing it right?', is a question haunting the prayers of many people, and it is nearly always answered in the negative. We start to feel guilty about the quantity and even more the quality of our praying, and guilt becomes a new hindrance to our access to God's grace. Those of us who try to help others on these matters, and who know our own hearts, will recognise how dominating anxiety and guilt can be and how they can take most of the joy out of praying.

This, in turn, can easily lead to an over-concern with techniques of prayer arising from a self-conscious concentration on ourselves and how we are doing in our efforts to reach God, rather than a liberating concentration on God himself, allowing us escape from ourselves. We have all met people for whom prayer has become a search for new, exotic ways of making it with God. They are seemingly for ever making brave new starts with prayer disciplines, whether charismatic or meditative, which tend to end in debilitating disappointments when the techniques are found incapable of delivering what they promised. The techniques and disciplines are useful tools when we are praying in the Spirit; when we trust them instead of the Spirit, they will certainly fail us.

A more Protestant version of this model of prayer makes faith the qualifying condition of its effectiveness. Only if we have enough faith of the right kind shall we make contact with God and enter into the fulfilment of his promises to us. If, after we have prayed with what faith we can muster, the answers do not come, we easily conclude that the fault was ours: we did not believe enough or expect enough and we are thrown back once more not on God's grace, but on our own failure in faith and the guilt and even despair that always generates in us. We need to remember that Jesus promised that faith which is no bigger than a grain of mustard seed is in a position to issue orders to mountains (Matt 17:21), because the important thing about faith is not how much you believe but in whom you believe.

Implicit in this model is the concept of blessing-centredness. Because the starting point of prayer is in ourselves and the power of prayer is the power of our own faith, it is not surprising that the purpose and reward of prayer should be seen as its ability to give us what we seek. Communion with God begins to be valued not in and for itself, but as a means of receiving what we and others need and which only God can give. The central test of the validity of prayer easily becomes: 'Did you get what you asked?'

The sixteenth-century Reformers would have called what we have just been describing a legal view of prayer. Prayer is seen in terms of law: it is a required human task to be carried out by disciplined human effort which will be rewarded, when it is done well, by generous divine response. Since the gospel does not abolish law but fulfils it, there is much in this model that we need to affirm, especially its insistence that prayer is too important to be left to passing whims and moods. It is a central controlling factor in our relationship with God to be undertaken with regularity and disciplined responsibility.

The trouble, however, with a law of prayer and indeed with all law, as Paul discovered, is that it is unaccomplishable on its own terms. It starts with man instead of with God; it puts its trust in man's effort rather than in God's grace; it aims at the blessings God can give rather than at God himself. If we come to prayer with no other resources than our own efforts to fulfil God's requirements, it should not surprise us if we either fail to persevere, or if our perseverance becomes burdensome duty from which expectancy has long since departed. Most of us would have to confess that we have known what it is like to belong to congregations whose worship is as dull and unhopeful as that, and that there have been times when our own praying has been no better. By the grace of God there have been other times when our experience of public worship and private prayer have been gloriously better than the gloomy picture we have been painting. Yet the picture has been worth looking at in some detail, because it helps us to identify where our praying has gone wrong, and where, perhaps more than anything else about us, it needs to be renewed by the Holy Spirit.

Prayer as Gift

In making our transition from this legal model of prayer to a very different and much more promising one, it is helpful to note what Paul says in Romans 8:26, which, along with the whole passage in which it is set, is the scriptural foundation for all that is to follow. 'We do not even know how to pray as we ought, but the Spirit comes to the aid of our weakness.' It is encouraging to us lesser mortals to see that even Paul starts from a recognition of much weakness and incapacity precisely in relation to prayer, the central point of our relationship to God. For the apostle prayer involves experiences of being at a loss either in regard to content, *what* to pray for, or in regard to method, *how* to pray for it.

It is the sort of dilemma that we all know well. If I have prayed for the healing of a sick friend and no healing has come, is it because I failed to discern God's will in the situation and, therefore, asked for the wrong thing? Or is it because I did not ask in the right way, not often enough, believingly enough, expectantly enough? We have all faced such imponderable questions about our praying, and it is good to know that Paul faced them too.

It is even better to take note of how Paul copes with this situation. He neither offers us new techniques by which to discover God's will nor exhorts us to new faith to let it be effected. Instead of being told to do something, we are directed to a source of help in prayer that comes to us from outside ourselves and our human resources, namely to the Holy Spirit. 'It is the Spirit who comes to the aid of our weakness.' This appeal to the Holy Spirit moves us from the model of prayer we have been describing to a quite different one. We are invited to see prayer not primarily as a duty required of us, but much more as a gift given to us by the Holy Spirit: God on our side of the relationship. Paul does not speak of what we ourselves are to do about our praying, but rather of what God is doing about it on our behalf.

That does not mean that there is no need for planned and disciplined activity by us in prayer and worship, but it makes that discipline a hopeful and expectant exercise, because at its basis is not our own effortfulness but our reliance on the divine help of the Spirit. Just as in Philippians 2:12–13 we can be told to work out our own salvation, precisely because God is willing and working his good pleasure within us, so in the context of worship we can work out our liturgies of worship and our disciplines of prayer just because the Holy Spirit is already at work in us. In both cases the divine activity in us is the presupposition of the human activity, rather than the other way round. It is not that we pray so that the Spirit can work in us; it is because the Spirit is already at work within us that we can pray. Among the choicest gifts of the Holy Spirit is the gift of prayer.

This is by no means an exclusively Pauline insight within the New Testament. According to Luke 11:1–13 something very like it goes right back to Jesus himself. The disciples, both daunted and attracted by Jesus' own practice of prayer and feeling the same inadequacy that Paul was to express later, approach him with their request: 'Lord, teach us to pray' (v 1). What he gave them in response to that request was the gift of a prayer not a course of instruction in prayer: 'When you pray, say, Father . . .' (v 2).

The Lord's prayer is not only a verbal formula to be repeated, but also the expression of a whole new relationship to God, his name, his will and his kingdom. Within this relationship as it is established and revealed by Jesus, characteristically Christian prayer becomes possible. The Lord makes us a gift of prayer which gives expression to the fact that we are adopted into sharing his own relationship to God, as sons and daughters to a Father. Furthermore, it is the Spirit whom the Father is willing to give to those who ask him (v 12), who prays the prayer given by Jesus within us, so that we can pray it not indeed by ourselves, but for ourselves, because the Spirit is enablingly at work within us.

Returning to Paul, it is very helpful to look at how he develops his teaching about prayer in Romans 8, because it gives us valuable clues as to what it means that prayer is a gift of the Holy Spirit before it is a task and discipline for us to perform.

First of all, Paul invites us to recognise that *we are prayed for*. According to Romans 8:34 (linking up at this point with one of the central insights of the Epistle to the Hebrews – see 7:25), prayer is the central activity of the ascended Jesus, 'who is at the right hand of God and is also interceding for us.' His ascension is not his retiral from his saving work; it is his entering into a new phase of it by his occupation of the place of authority at the right hand of God. This king who reigns is also a priest who prays; he reigns, so to speak, from his knees. The universal power he exercises is not supernatural brute force; it is the power of his once-and-for-all self-giving on Calvary, the power of the sacrificing love in which he offered himself to his Father on behalf of the sins of the world.

It is not that he pleads with a Father who is reluctant to give. Intercession in a Christian context is never a matter of persuading God to give what he would otherwise withhold. Rather, all authentically divine power is released through self-giving – the self-giving of the Father to the Son in the Spirit and the responsive self-giving of the Son to the Father in the same Spirit. What the cross demonstrates for ever is that with God power is self-giving, and self-giving is power. This is why intercession, first Christ's and then ours in him, is effective. When we pray for others we walk again the way of the cross and offer ourselves to God on their behalf. As Christ offered himself as an atoning sacrifice for the sins of the world, in a way that neither can nor needs to be repeated, so we offer ourselves in and through him, so that the benefits of his saving work may be applied to others.

Now in heaven Jesus, the great high priest, gives himself to the Father in intercession on our behalf. He does it as one of us who has plumbed the depths of our need and our misery and on the cross has offered to God an atoning obedience. He does it as the one who knows that the Father has responded to his atoning self-giving by raising him from the dead, and that he will, therefore, respond to his priestly intercession by giving him what he asks for us. His is the prayer of the great Mediator, who is both God and man. He knows from the inside both the gracious divine purpose and the disgraced human situation and by his intercession can expose the one to the other.

Therefore, whether we ourselves pray well or badly, the perfect prayer on our behalf is continually being offered by the Son to the Father in the Spirit. That puts our frustration about our own praying into a new and far more positive perspective. It does not all depend on us and the quantity and quality of our own devotional performance, whether together or alone. As Jesus vicariously and efficaciously died for us on the cross, so he now vicariously and efficaciously prays for us as the ascended Lord. Our own praying is significant and acceptable not in its own strength or inherent excellence, but only in its association and identification with his praying for us and with us. 'Through Christ we have access in one Spirit to the Father' (Eph 2:18). We pray always and only through Jesus Christ our Lord.

Luke provides the perfect illustration. On Maundy Thursday in the upper room Jesus addresses the far too self-confident Peter who is promising to go with him to prison and to death, 'Simon, Simon, Satan has asked to sift you as wheat. But *I have prayed for you*, Simon, that your faith may not fail' (Luke 22:31–32). If Peter's faith and apostleship survived his threefold denial of Jesus, the secret of that survival was not anything in Peter himself, but the intercession of Jesus on his behalf. This is, indeed, the central secret of all Christian survival, progress and victory. It counteracts and overcomes all the inadequacies and infidelities that burden our own prayers – 'I have prayed for you.'

Not only are we prayed for by the ascended Son, but *we are prayed in by the indwelling Spirit*. Perfect intercession is going on not only at the heart of heaven where Christ prays, but in our own hearts where the Spirit prays. 'We do not know what we ought to pray for, but the Spirit pleads for us with groans that words cannot express. And he who searches our hearts knows the mind of the Spirit, because the Spirit intercedes for the saints in accordance with God's will' (Rom 8:26–7).

On the surface our prayer is often at the level of inarticulate groans to God, but in the depths of us, the Spirit God has given us through Christ is praying the perfect prayer that we cannot pray on our own, and the Father hears and responds to the prayer of his own Spirit in us. These are words of the utmost mystery and profundity that Paul does not stop to explain. However, they most certainly indicate an understanding of the work and person of the Spirit which is in harmony with what we have been presenting throughout this book. The Spirit, as the one who intercedes for us, is personally distinguished from the Father to whom he prays. Equally as the one who prays in our hearts, he is also distinguished from the Son who prays at the right hand of the Father. Here in the context of prayer, we can see a still undeveloped but very impressively real approach to a trinitarian understanding of God.[3]

Even more important in our present context, what the Spirit does is to bring over to our side of the relationship the Father's self-giving to the Son and the Son's self-giving to the Father, which, as we have seen, are the very heart and centre of intercession. The Spirit is himself that self-giving in person, and he enables us both to receive what the Father gives us through the Son, and to be caught up into the priestly self-giving of the Son to the Father on behalf of others. As the Spirit takes the love and power of Christ with which he serves the Father and makes them ours, so also he takes the intercessory prayer of Christ in heaven and makes it ours here on earth.

In the Spirit we pray Christ's perfect prayer with him. Christ prays for us before we pray for ourselves, but he keeps nothing to himself. He invites and enables us to participate in all that he has and does, including his prayer. Through his self-giving to his Father's purposes the world is both created and redeemed. When the Spirit prays in us and we pray in the Spirit, we are caught up into Christ's self-offering to the Father, who in response to our prayer does the creative and redemptive things that further his purposes in those for whom we pray.

To speak as we have done is of course to go far beyond what Paul actually says so tantalisingly briefly in Romans 8. I would, however, maintain that his words point quite clearly, if still implicitly, in the direction of the sort of trinitarian understanding of prayer that we have just been outlining, in which the Spirit enables us to participate in the dynamic and creative interchange of love between the Father and his ascended Son.

Of course the main lessons of Paul's teaching here are for our spiritual practice rather than for our trinitarian theology. These have been memorably expounded by André Louf in his book *Teach us to Pray* which has been a major influence behind the thinking in this chapter and in my own approach to the life of prayer in recent years. If the theology of baptism implied in the quotation that follows is not to the liking of all of us, it is not hard to translate it in terms of a different understanding of when and how the Christian life begins and still take affirmative account of the main point that Louf is making.

'We received prayer along with grace in our baptism. The state of grace, as we call it, at the level of the heart actually signifies a *state of prayer*. From then on in the profoundest depths of the self, we have a continuing contact with God. God's Holy Spirit has taken us over, has assumed complete possession of us; he has become breath of our breath and Spirit of our spirit. He takes our heart in tow and turns it towards God ... This state of prayer within us is something we always carry about with us, like a hidden treasure of which we are not consciously aware. Somewhere our heart is going full pelt, but we do not feel it. We are deaf to our praying heart.'[4]

The prayer of the Spirit, which is first the prayer of Christ in heaven, is being offered to the Father in our hearts. This is the gift of prayer that was given when the Spirit himself was given, that is, when our relationship to Christ began. Yet, like many other gifts of the Spirit, it was given then but it may not have been consciously received then. It is perfectly possible to be largely unaware of the prayer life the Spirit has given us and try by our own efforts to manufacture one of our own.

The practical implications of this second approach to prayer are of the most positive kind. We are not the prayerless people we often take ourselves to be. We carry prayer within us, because the praying Spirit is within us. We do not need ourselves to produce prayer or the faith which gives it access to God. Prayer and the confidence with which to approach God are given to us by the Spirit who cries *Abba*, Father, within us, and who directs us away from ourselves to Christ in and with whom we give ourselves to God.

God is not just out there waiting for our prayers and leaving it to us to find the right techniques and the required faith by which to reach him. Jesus is not just the perfect example of prayer that daunts us by his very perfection and our often proved inability to pray as he did. God the Holy Spirit is on our side of the relationship, shaping and inspiring our response to the Father and the Son, showing us what and how to pray, enabling us to join in the intercession of Christ himself.

We can apply Paul's statement in Galatians 2:20 about Christian life in general to this particular context. 'It is no longer I that *pray* but Christ that *prays* in me.' Before, therefore, we ourselves begin to pray, we are to listen until we hear how the Spirit is praying within us and among us. If we are open to him, the Spirit will enable us to pray with the discernment and the trusting faith with which the Son intercedes with the Father. We must receive the prayer from God the Spirit, before we can be identified with God the Son in offering it to God the Father. The thought of receiving prayer from God before we offer it to God is not strange to those of us who use the Anglican liturgies where morning and evening prayer both begin with the sentences from the

Psalms: 'O Lord, open thou our lips; and our mouths shall show forth thy praise.'

The first priority in prayer is therefore to listen, so that, even if we start by asking for what we want, we shall be open, as we pray, to have the Spirit reshape the content of our prayer to bring it into harmony with what Christ is praying on our behalf. Jesus himself in Gethsemane began by asking that the cup of atoning suffering might pass from him: 'My Father, if it is possible, let this cup be taken from me' (Matt 26:39). As he prayed, the Spirit of his Father in him reshaped his discernment of God's purpose in the situation he was facing, so that his prayer itself changed: 'My Father, if it is not possible for this cup to be taken away until I drink it, may your will be done' (v 42). Through his prayer he is ready now to go where *Abba* sends him and drink what *Abba* gives him.

What the Spirit does in the humanity of Jesus he also does in ours. We begin to pray for what seems good to us, but we become aware of another personal participant on our side of the exchange with God, sharing with us quite different perspectives on the situation we are concerned with, and persuading us to pray different prayers in the light of what he shows us. It happens in personal prayer; it happens even more when we pray together in an open way in groups. It is the action of the Spirit interceding for the saints in accordance with God's will.

When, for example, we begin to pray for a seriously ill friend, we shall start, as Jesus did in Gethsemane, by asking for what we naturally and rightly want for him – his full and complete recovery. Yet we shall do so, again like Jesus, tentatively and conditionally, listening all the time for the Spirit to initiate us into God's immediate and particular will for our friend. God's ultimate purpose for him will indeed be complete wholeness, but we need to learn in each situation whether the appointed way to that wholeness is to be by recovery, by continuing weakness in which God can perfect his strength, as with Paul in II Corinthians 12:9, or even through death to the body leading to resurrection. All these are on God's agenda and it is the Spirit who will show us in

each case how we are to pray – for a marvellous healing, for
grace to endure, for a good death.

The perfect prayer of the Spirit in us will always to some
extent be transcendent to our hearing of it. Our own loves
and longings can keep us from discerning the mind of the
Spirit, and even when they do not, there will always remain in
the prayer of the Spirit that which is beyond our grasp and
that therefore we cannot utter. Perhaps the gift of tongues is
one expression of how the Spirit's prayer is beyond our
understanding and our speaking. When we pray in the Spirit,
we pray past ourselves and beyond ourselves. What God
hears and answers is not the imperfect prayer that comes
from our lips but the prayer of the Spirit that rises from our
deepest hearts. 'He who searches our hearts knows the mind
of the Spirit.' God does not answer only when we ask aright,
as man-centred arminian approaches to prayer often suggest.
'He is able to do immeasurably more than all we ask or
imagine according to his power that is at work within us'
(Eph 3:20).

The Spirit's help in prayer and worship is by no means
confined to particular discernments of God's will in specific
acts of intercession. He does not only inspire prayer in the
heart: he gives a heritage of prayer and praise to the whole
Christian community. The discernment of the mind of the
Spirit which is also the mind of the Father and of the Son is to
be sought primarily and normatively in the apostolic
Scriptures which the Spirit has inspired. Anything that
contradicts or denies the given gospel is not the gift of the
Spirit.

The Spirit's gift of worship is also offered to us through the
Church's liturgy, in so far as it is an authentic response to the
scriptural gospel. The worship of the Church of the past is the
Spirit's gift to the Church of the present, if we will use it not as
external ritual, but as that which the Spirit has once owned
and will again enliven for us. Many of us have been grateful
for the communion we have found with God through the
prayers of the Church's liturgy on days when we had no
prayer of our own.

The more we remain in fellowship with the prayers of the

saints who have gone before us, the more open we shall be to the new things that the Spirit is doing in the Church of today. It is through our fellowship in prayer with those who belong to different ages and different cultures that the Spirit will teach us to discern his work and gifts from the fashions of the hour and the self-deceivings of our own hearts.

The Spirit will be known both for his faithfulness to the gospel and for his contemporary creativity and spontaneity. He who created a praiseful worship of the Father and the Son in ways that were authentic to all the cultures and centuries in which the gospel has been confessed, will do the same in new ways that are authentic to the end of the twentieth century. The prayer of the Spirit will be liturgical, in continuity with what has gone before, but it will also be free, creative and spontaneous. Both those who cannot worship except with raised hands, charismatic choruses and guitars, and those who cannot worship except through venerable liturgies speaking in the language and thought-forms of three hundred years ago, fall short of the fullness of the Spirit who produces treasures old and new by which the Church can glorify the Father and what he has done for us in his Son.

* * *

It is good that we should end in the context of worship, because it is there that we enter most deeply into the unfathomable mystery of the triune God, which is far beyond all our words and all our thinking. It is there that the Holy Spirit of whom we have been speaking is most himself; it is there that his oneness with and his personal distinction from the Father and the Son are most clearly revealed; it is there that we enter most fully into the life of God, where Father and Son give themselves to each other in the Spirit who proceeds from the Father to the Son.

In the Holy Spirit that self-giving love, in which alone God is God, opens itself up to us. The Gift who is the Spirit is God himself in gracious personal presence on our side of the relationship. He is the Giving Gift, because he enables us to share in the life and the love in which the Father, the Son and

Eastern mentality

the Spirit have from all eternity had their being. By his Son and his Spirit, the two hands of God, the Father embraces his prodigal children and draws them to himself. The Spirit who brought the Son into life-sharing oneness with us, has begun to bring us through that Son into life-sharing oneness with the triune God, to whom be glory for ever.

Notes on Chapter Nine

(1) I find this understanding of atonement as priestly intercession extremely helpful. It was a central notion for J. McLeod Campbell in *The Nature of the Atonement*, (London, Macmillan, Sixth edition 1915, Chapter 5, esp p 127ff), was further developed in dialogue with more traditional evangelical views by P.T. Forsyth in *The Work of Christ*, (London, Independent Press, 1910, esp Chapter 5) and in the contemporary writings of T.F. Torrance e.g. *Theology in Reconciliation*, (London, Geoffrey Chapman, 1975, Chapter Three, 106–114.

(2) For what immediately follows I am much indebted to my friend, Professor J.B. Torrance of Aberdeen; cf. his article 'The Vicarious Humanity of Christ' in *The Incarnation*, T.F. Torrance ed., Edinburgh, Handsel Press, 1981, pp 127–30.

(3) This approach to the Trinity through the experience of prayer has recently been expounded in a most helpful way in the Report of the Church of England Doctrine Commission, starting from these verses in Romans 8. (*We Believe in God*, London, Church House Publishing 1987, Chapter 7, pp 104–121).

(4) André Louf, *Teach us to Pray*, London, Darton, Longman & Todd, 1974, pp 18–19.
cf also Yves Congar, *I Believe in the Holy Spirit*, (ET, London, Geoffrey Chapman, 1983, Vol II, Chapter 5 esp pp 115–7.)

Index

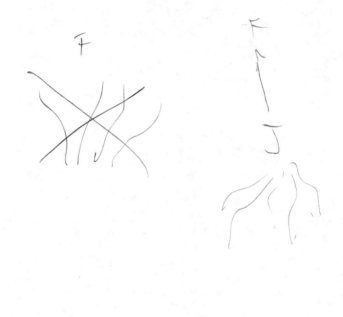